Christmas Incarnation

A Study of Jesus' Birth
and of Mary, Joseph, Angels, and the Wise Men

for Personal Use, Small Groups or Sunday School
Classes, and Sermon Preparation for Pastors and Teachers

JesusWalk® Bible Study Series

Ralph F. Wilson
Director, Joyful Heart Renewal Ministries

Free Question Handout Sheets

www.jesuswalk.com/christmas-incarnation/christmas-incarnation-questions.pdf

Additional Books, DVDs and Reprint Licenses

www.jesuswalk.com/books/christmas-incarnation.htm

JesusWalk® Publications
www.jesuswalk.com/books/
Loomis, California

Copyright © 2007, 2011, Ralph F. Wilson. All rights reserved. May not be copied or reproduced without explicit permission.

ISBN-13: 978-0-9832310-3-5
ISBN-10: 0983231036

Library of Congress Control Number: 2011906551
Library of Congress subject headings:
  Jesus Christ – Nativity.
  Bible. – N.T. – Matthew I-II – Criticism, interpretation, etc.
  Bible. – N.T. – Luke I-II – Criticism, interpretation, etc.
Suggested Classifications:
  Library of Congress: BT315
  Dewey Decimal: 232.92

Published by JesusWalk® Publications, P.O. Box 565, Loomis, CA 95650, USA. JesusWalk.com

JesusWalk is a registered trademark and Joyful Heart is a trademark of Joyful Heart Renewal Ministries.

Unless otherwise stated, quotations are from the New International Version (International Bible Society, 1973, 1978, 1983). Used by permission.

110428

Preface

Sir Anthony Van Dyck (Flemish painter, 1599-1641), "Madonna of the Straw," Galleria Nazionale d'Arte Antica, Rome.

The coming of God into this world to be a man – the incarnation – must figure among the greatest events in all human history. Yet in our over-Christmased culture we have trivialized the true Nativity Story in favor of images of Santa and gushings about the warmth of the true Christmas spirit.

This four-lesson series is designed to help us reconnect with the real meaning of Christmas by considering one-by-one the main characters of the Christmas story:

1. Mary
2. Joseph
3. The Shepherds
4. The Wise Men

Each was a disciple of Jesus – St. Mary, the – first disciple, followed one-by-one by the others who recognized this newborn as the Messiah and reordered their lives around Him as a result.

This is an old story – one we've heard in countless sermons. But re-examining it in thoughtful detail from Scripture will help us re-experience its power and truth.

Christmas, of course, is not at its core about spiced cider, gaily-wrapped presents, and shining ornaments. It is about the incarnation, the in-fleshment of the Son of God as a human being. This story did not take place in a decorated villa of Nazareth or a sterilized stable in Bethlehem. The story unfolded among real people whom God called for a purpose beyond themselves – and who responded, "Yes," when called. It is a story of discipleship and risk. Of faith and hope. Of intimate, caring love and bold never-to-turn-back decisions. The true story of Christmas has the power to re-ignite living faith in us and deepen the quality of our discipleship.

It is my prayer that this Christmas the gutsy faith of the central characters in this wonderful story will call forth in us a bold trust in response, that we too might be faithful, solid players in the great drama God is bringing about in our own twenty-first century world.

Dr. Ralph F. Wilson
Loomis, California
October 20, 2007

Table of Contents

Preface	3
Table of Contents	5
References and Abbreviations	8
Reprint Guidelines	10
1. Mary, the Virgin Mother (Luke 1:26-45)	12
The Facts of Mary's Life (Luke 1:26-27)	13
Mary's Alarm (Luke 1:28-30)	15
The Angel's Unparalleled Announcement (Lk 1:31-33)	16
The Wonder in Mary's Mind (Luke 1:34)	19
Conceived by the Holy Spirit (Luke 1:35)	21
The Meaning of the Incarnation	22
Nothing is Impossible with God (Luke 1:36-37)	23
Mary's Amazing Submission (Luke 1:38)	25
Blessed Mother of God (Luke 1:42-45)	27
2. Joseph, the Stand-In Father (Matthew 1:18-25)	31
Joseph's Name	33
Joseph the Husband	33
Joseph the Carpenter	34
Mary's Predicament, Joseph's Dilemma	36
Joseph, the Righteous Man (Matthew 1:19)	38
The Angel's Revelation in a Dream (Matthew 1:20-21)	41
The Name "Jesus" (Matthew 1:21)	42
Joseph Shall Adopt the Child (Matthew 1:21)	44

The Virgin Will Conceive (Matthew 1:22-23)	44
Emmanuel, God with Us (Matthew 1:23)	47
Joseph's Obedience (Matthew 1:24-25)	48
Joseph Protects Jesus (Matthew 2:13-15)	49
3. The Shepherds' Sign of the Manger (Luke 2:1-20)	**52**
1. Jesus Is Born in History (Luke 2:1-2)	53
2. Jesus Is Born in David's Birthplace (Luke 2:3-4)	54
3. Jesus' Birth Is Attended by Hardship (Luke 2:5-6)	56
4. Jesus Is Born in Humble Circumstances (Luke 2:7)	57
Shepherds Keeping Watch over Their Flocks (Luke 2:8)	58
The Glory of the Lord (Luke 2:9)	61
The Good News Angel (Luke 2:10-11)	62
A Savior (Luke 2:11)	64
Christ the Lord (Luke 2:11)	64
At the Sign of a Manger (Luke 2:12)	66
Glory to God in the Highest (Luke 2:13-14)	67
The Shepherd's Response (Luke 2:15-18)	68
Mary Ponders the Shepherd's Report (Luke 2:19)	69
Joyful Shepherds (Luke 2:20)	70
Lessons for Disciples	71
4. Wise Men and the Christmas Star of Bethlehem (Matthew 2:1-12)	**73**
Who Are the Magi? (Matthew 2:1)	74
What Kind of "Star" Did They See? (Matthew 2:2)	75
Why Was Herod Disturbed? (Matthew 2:3)	78
Where Was the Messiah to Be Born? (Matthew 2:4-6)	79
Herod's Plot (Matthew 2:7-8)	80
Led by the Star (Matthew 2:9-10)	81
Worshipping the King (Matthew 2:11a)	82
Offering Gifts to the King (Matthew 2:11b)	84
Disobeying Herod (Matthew 2:12)	87
What Does All this Mean?	88

Appendix: Class Handouts	92
1. Mary, the Virgin Mother (Luke 1:26-45)	93
2. Joseph, the Stand-In Father (Matthew 1:18-25)	95
3. The Shepherds' Sign of the Manger (Luke 2:1-20)	97
4. Wise Men and the Christmas Star of Bethlehem (Matthew 2:1-12)	99

References and Abbreviations

BDAG   Walter Bauer and Frederick W. Danker, *A Greek-English Lexicon of the New Testament and Other Early Christian Literature* (Third Edition; based on a previous English edition by W.F. Arndt, F.W. Gingrich, and F.W. Danker; University of Chicago Press, 1957, 1979, 2001).

Brown   Raymond E. Brown, *The Birth of the Messiah: A Commentary on the Infancy Narratives of Matthew and Luke* (Updated edition; Anchor Bible Reference Library; Doubleday, 1977, 1993)

DJG   Joel B. Green, Scot McKnight, I. Howard Marshall (editors), *Dictionary of Jesus and the Gospels* (InterVarsity Press, 1992)

Green   Joel B. Green, *The Gospel of Luke* (The New International Commentary on the New Testament; Eerdmans, 1997)

ISBE   Geoffrey W. Bromiley (general editor), *The International Standard Bible Encyclopedia* (Eerdmans, 1979-1988; fully revised from the 1915 edition)

Life &   Alfred Edersheim, *The Life and Times of*

Times	*Jesus the Messiah* (2 volume edition; Eerdmans, 1969, reprinted from the third edition, 1886)
Marshall	I. Howard Marshall, *Commentary on Luke* (New International Greek Testament Commentary; Eerdmans, 1978)
Morris, *Luke*	Leon Morris, *The Gospel According to St. Luke* (Tyndale NT Commentaries; Eerdmans, 1974)
Morris, *Matthew*	Leon Morris, *The Gospel According to Matthew* (Pillar Commentary series; Eerdmans, 1992)
Strack and Billerbeck	H.L. Strack und P. Billerbeck, *Kommentar zum Neuen Testament aus Talmud und Midrasch* (München, 1956)
TDNT	Gerhard Kittel and Gerhard Friedrich (editors), Geoffrey W. Bromiley (translator and editor), *Theological Dictionary of the New Testament* (Eerdmans, 1964-1976; ten volume edition)
TWOT	R. Laird Harris, Gleason L. Archer, Jr., and Bruce K. Waltke, editors), *Theological Wordbook of the Old Testament* (2 volumes, Moody Press, 1980)

Reprint Guidelines

Copying the Handouts. In some cases, small groups or Sunday school classes would like to use these notes to study this material. That's great. An appendix provides copies of handouts designed for classes and small groups. There is no charge whatsoever to print out as many copies of the handouts as you need for participants. Or print them in 8-1/2 x 11" format from

www.jesuswalk.com/christmas-incarnation/christmas-incarnation-questions.pdf

All charts and notes are copyrighted and must bear the line:

"Copyright © 2011, Ralph F. Wilson. All rights reserved. Reprinted by permission."

You may not resell these notes to other groups or individuals outside your congregation. You may, however, charge people in your group enough to cover your copying costs.

Copying the book (or the majority of it) in your congregation or group, you are requested to purchase a reprint license for each book. A Reprint License, $1.50 for each copy is available for purchase at

www.jesuswalk.com/books/christmas-incarnation.htm

Or you may send a check to:

Dr. Ralph F. Wilson
JesusWalk Publications
PO Box 565
Loomis, CA 95650, USA

The Scripture says,

"The laborer is worthy of his hire" (Luke 10:7) and "Anyone who receives instruction in the word must share all good things with his instructor" (Galatians 6:6).

However, if you are from a third world country or an area where it is difficult to transmit money, please make a small contribution instead to help the poor in your community.

1. Mary, the Virgin Mother (Luke 1:26-45)

"Virgin Mother!" If it seems like a contradiction in terms, an oxymoron, to us, what do you think it seemed like to Mary, that young teenager who had thrust upon her the most momentous birth in the history of the world? Virgin mother.

A detailed examination of Mary's whole life throughout the Bible is beyond the scope of our study.

Dante Gabriel Rossetti, "Ecce Ancilla Domini (The Annunciation" (1849-50), oil on canvas, 28-1/2 x 16-1/2 in, Tate Gallery, London

We'll focus on two incidents that are central to the Christmas theme of the birth of Jesus – the Annunciation and Mary's visit to her cousin Elizabeth. They give us some wonderful insights into Mary's heart and her faith and provide inspiration to our own spiritual lives, and they help us understand Jesus' divine nature better, as well.

1. Mary, the Virgin Mother (Luke 1:26-45)

Before we begin, let me introduce Mary as St. Mary. The title may shock Protestant Christians, who rightly consider all believers as saints, but she has been known to the Church by this honorary title of "saint" for two millennia – and for good reason. She has encouraged literally millions of Christians by her love for God, her submission to his will, and her willingness to see through to the end the path chosen for her by the Most High. So let's consider St. Mary together.

Luke's account of the Annunciation (Luke 1:26-30), that is the angel's "announcement" to Mary of her mission of motherhood, tells us a number of things about Mary. It begins with the basic facts of her life.

The Facts of Mary's Life (Luke 1:26-27)

> "In the sixth month, God sent the angel Gabriel to Nazareth, a town in Galilee, to a virgin pledged to be married to a man named Joseph, a descendant of David. The virgin's name was Mary." (Luke 1:26-27)

The angel "sent"[1] from God is Gabriel, which means "God's valiant one."[2] He is no newcomer to the pages of Scripture. He had been sent in "swift flight" to the prophet Daniel (Daniel 9:21; 8:16). He was sent to speak to John the Baptist's father Zechariah while he was ministering in the temple of God

---

[1] *Apostellō*, "to dispatch someone for the achievement of some objective, send out, send away" (BDAG, 120-121, 1bδ).

[2] *Gabriēl*, BDAG 186. It is a Hebrew compound word from *geber*, "mighty man" + *'ēl*, "God." *Geber* is from the verb *gābar*, "prevail, be mighty, have strength, be great" (John N. Oswalt, *gābar*, TWOT #310).

(Luke 1:11-20) and told him, "I am Gabriel. I stand in the presence of God" (1:19). This awesome, mighty angelic messenger must have been fearsome to behold.

The Angel's announcement takes place six months after Elizabeth becomes pregnant with John the Baptist. Mary lived in the village of Nazareth, in the hilly area southwest of the Sea of Galilee. We're also told that Mary was a virgin, betrothed but not yet married. This gives us some clues about her age, since we know that young women were usually betrothed at age twelve to twelve-and-a-half – a full year before the actual marriage ceremony took place. Mary was probably a very young teenager when God spoke to her.[3] Sometimes we discount the spiritual lives of young teens as immature, but God takes them very seriously.

Her husband-to-be is Joseph, a direct descendent of David, Israel's greatest king (Matthew 1:6-16; Luke 2:4). Mary's ancestry is more complex. Mary's relative Elizabeth was probably a descendent of the original high priest, Aaron, of the tribe of Levi (Luke 1:5). But some believe that Mary also may be a descendent

---

[3] Joachim Jeremias, *Jerusalem in the Time of Jesus* (Fortress Press, 1969, translated from the third German edition, 1962), p. 365, cites Strack and Billerbeck (II, 374), that the usual age for a girl's betrothal was between twelve and twelve and a half. He cites *M.Ket.* v.2 that the marriage itself ordinarily took place one year after betrothal.

herself of David of the tribe of Judah on her father's side (1:32).[4]

Mary's Alarm (Luke 1:28-30)

> "The angel went to her and said, 'Greetings, you who are highly favored! The Lord is with you.' Mary was greatly troubled at his words and wondered what kind of greeting this might be. But the angel said to her, 'Do not be afraid, Mary, you have found favor with God.'" (Luke 1:28-30)

Gabriel, the mighty angel, comes with words that are so grand and magnanimous that they are suited to an appearance before royalty more than to a Nazareth peasant girl: "Greetings, you who are highly favored!" "Greetings" (NIV, NRSV) or "hail" is "a formalized greeting wishing one well,"[5] not uncommon in the New Testament. But calling her "highly favored"[6] is powerful praise. "The Lord is with you" are the same words the angel of the Lord spoke to Gideon (Judges 6:12).[7]

---

[4] Geoffrey W. Bromiley, "Mary," ISBE 3:269-273. The issue hinges on whether "of the house of David" in Luke 1:27 goes with "virgin" or "Joseph." See also Luke 1:32 and Acts 2:30, which seem to indicate a physical descent from David.

[5] *Chairō*, BDAG 1075, 2a.

[6] *Charitoō*, "to cause to be the recipient of a benefit, bestow favor on, favor highly, bless" (BDAG 1081), from *charis*, "favor, grace."

[7] The KJV adds at the end of 1:28 "blessed art thou among women," following ancient 'Greek manuscripts such as A C D Θ and the Textus Receptus. However, the words are omitted by a wide diversity of early texts, including Aleph B L W Ψ and others. Metzger says, "It is probably that copyists inserted [these words] here from verse 42, where 'they are firmly attested. If the clause had been original in the present verse, there is no adequate reason why it should have been omitted

If you were a young teen and heard an angel speak these words to you, about you, you'd be scared spitless. Luke says that Mary was greatly troubled. The Greek word is *diatarassō*, which means to "confuse, perplex."[8,9] Gabriel counters with the words "Do not be afraid, Mary," and Mary accepted the angel's "Fear not" at face value.

The Angel's Unparalleled Announcement (Luke 1:31-33)

Now comes the thrust of Gabriel's message:

> "'You will be with child and give birth to a son, and you are to give him the name Jesus. He will be great and will be called the Son of the Most High. The Lord God will give him the throne of his father David, and he will reign over the house of Jacob forever; his kingdom will never end.'" (Luke 1:31-34)

Sandro Botticelli, "Virgin and Child with Angel" (c. 1475), Chicago Institute of Art.

---

from a wide diversity of early witnesses" (Bruce M. Metzger, *A Textual Commentary on the Greek New Testament* (United Bible Societies, 1971), p. 129).

[8] *Diatarassō*, BDAG 237.

[9] *Phobeō*, "to be in an apprehensive state, be afraid, become frightened," from which we get our English word "phobia" (BDAG 1060-1062).

1. Mary, the Virgin Mother (Luke 1:26-45)

Notice the points of this announcement.
- Mary will become pregnant.
- Mary will give birth to a son.

The child must be given the name "Jesus," which we'll talk more about this when we study the angel's word to Joseph (Matthew 1:21).

The child will become a great person. *Megas* means "superior in importance, great, in high position."[10]

His title will be "Son of the Most High." God first revealed himself to Abraham as the Most High God (*'El 'Elyon*, Genesis 14:18-22). This title is used many times in Scripture.[11] "Son of" can mean literal biological or legal offspring, but as a Hebrew idiom it often carries the idea of "a person related or closely associated as if by ties of sonship, son."[12] A "son of perdition" (John 17:12; 2 Thessalonians 2:3) means the person who will go to perdition or destruction, "the man doomed to destruction" (NIV). "Sons of oil" (Zechariah 4:14) means "anointed ones," the term sons expressing their relationship to the anointing oil. The term "Son of God" in the New Testament refers to Jesus' close association with God himself, and is another way of referring to his divinity, "the only

---

[10] *Megas*, BDAG 623-624, 4a.

[11] Psalm 7:17; 18:13; 50:14; 57:2; 83:18; Micah 6:6; Luke 1:17; 2:14; 6:35; 8:28; Acts 7:48; 16:17; Hebrews 7:1. See my book *Names and Titles of God* (JesusWalk Publications, 2010), chapter 1.

[12] *Huios*, BDAG 1024-1027. Peter Wülfing von Martitz, Georg Fourer, Eduard Schweizer, Eduard Lohse, and Wilhelm Schneemelcher, *huios*, TDNT 8:334-392.

begotten of the Father" (John 1:14). To hear her son referred to as divine must have been overwhelming for Mary.

He will inherit "the throne of his father David, and he will reign over the house of Jacob forever," in other words, he will be the long anticipated King of the Jews, the Jewish Messiah, the "Son of David," who will reign over the Kingdom of God.

Finally, "his kingdom will never end." He will not just reign for a lifetime but forever. This is a clear though distant echo of God's original promise to David:

> "Your house and your kingdom will endure forever before me; your throne will be established forever." (2 Samuel 7:16).

But it is not just an enduring dynasty, it is an everlasting personal reign. The other antecedent is the "Son of Man" prophecy made to Daniel centuries before:

> "In my vision at night I looked, and there before me was one like a son of man, coming with the clouds of heaven. He approached the Ancient of Days and was led into his presence. He was given authority, glory and sovereign power; all peoples, nations and men of every language worshiped him. His dominion is an everlasting dominion that will not pass away, and his kingdom is one that will never be destroyed" (Daniel 7:13-14).

Jesus acknowledged before the high priest at his trial that he was indeed this heavenly Son of Man who will reign forever (Matthew 26:64) and it was on the basis of this statement that he was condemned for blasphemy.

Q1. (Luke 1:31-34) What did the angel's announcement say about who Mary's Child was and who he was to become?
http://www.joyfulheart.com/forums/index.php?showtopic=709

7|2

The Wonder in Mary's Mind (Luke 1:34)

What fascinates me is Mary's interior life. I imagine that Mary's head was spinning by this time, though I'm sure she didn't take time to examine in detail all seven points of the angel's announcement. It was the first one that had to do with her – "You will be with child..." (1:31a) – that prompted her question:

> "'How will this be,' Mary asked the angel, 'since I am a virgin?'" (Luke 1:34)

Mary's words in Greek don't use the word for "virgin" (*parthenos*, 1:26), but translated literally are: "... seeing I know (*ginoskō*) not a man...." (KJV). What does she mean?

1. This couldn't happen because I'm not intimate with a man; or

2. How will God accomplish this, since the normal means of pregnancy isn't available?

What the Angel announced was supernatural. A miracle. The response can be either: (1) Miracles just don't happen, so prove it to me, as Zechariah had responded to an angel's announcement in the temple (1:18), the response of unbelief. Or it could be: (2) Wow! That's amazing! How will it happen? – the response of wonder and faith.

Some people say we shouldn't question God, but Mary did. She asked "How?" Questions cause us to grow and learn. Questions stretch our minds and hearts and increase our understanding. Questions and the exploration for their answers contribute to our faith, even if the questions themselves may ultimately go unanswered. Mary's question arose from faith, not doubt. What would your response to the Angel be? Faith or unbelief?

Q2. (Luke 1:34) In what way does Mary's "How?" question (1:34) to the angel's declaration differ from Zechariah's "How?" question (1:18)? Why was Mary rewarded and Zechariah disciplined?
http://www.joyfulheart.com/forums/index.php?showtopic=710

Conceived by the Holy Spirit (Luke 1:35)

The angel responded to her sincere question by elaborating a bit on the "how":

> "The angel answered, 'The Holy Spirit will come upon you, and the power of the Most High will overshadow you. So the holy one to be born will be called the Son of God.'" (Luke 1:35)

The angel explains delicately that the Holy Spirit "will come upon you" (*eperchomai*), not in a sexual way but in the same way as the Holy Spirit came upon the disciples in the upper room on the Day of Pentecost (see Acts 1:8) where this same word is used of the Holy Spirit. Two other analogies in the New Testament to describe a coming of the Holy Spirit upon a person are "filled" and "baptized." The Spirit transforms people!

The angel is speaking in a kind of poetic form that you see in Hebrew poetry, such as in the Psalms and the prophets. The first line makes a statement and the second line says the same thing in other words. Hebrew scholars call this poetic form "synoptic parallelism":

> "The Holy Spirit will come upon you,
> and the power of the Most High
> will overshadow you..." (Luke 1:35)

"The power of the Most High" is another way of saying "Holy Spirit," while "overshadow" (*episkiazō*) is another way of saying "come upon."

The purpose of the Holy Spirit's coming is, "... So the holy one to be born will be called the Son of God" (1:35c). This sentence describes the mystery of the incarnation – the divine becoming joined with the human.

Mary is human, but her child, conceived by the Holy Spirit, is "holy" in the same sense that God himself is holy. What's more, this human-divine child will be called the Son of God. This is not just a figurative use of the Hebrew idiom "son of," meaning "closely associated with." It is quite clear that Luke intended for us to see this pregnancy and birth as a divine miracle, and the child as the biological (if that word has any meaning here) offspring of God *and* Mary.

The Meaning of the Incarnation

Christians call this the incarnation, from the Latin *in-* + *carn-*, *caro*, "flesh." It is a wonderful mystery. The early church Fathers struggled to describe it. The Apostle's Creed (as early as the second century, Rome) puts it simply:

> "I believe ... in Jesus Christ, his only Son, our Lord, who was conceived by the Holy Spirit, born of the Virgin Mary...."

The Nicene Creed (325, 391 AD) spells out the implications of the virgin birth with greater clarity:

> "We believe ... in one Lord Jesus Christ, the only-begotten Son of God, begotten of the Father before all worlds, Light of Light, very God of very God,

begotten, not made, being of one substance with the Father...."

The Nicene Fathers used an interesting Greek word, *homoousios*, "of the **same** nature" or "of the **same** essence," translated as "one substance" in our English translations. *Homoousios*, "same nature, same essence" was the terminology adopted by the Council of Nicea in 325 AD to describe Jesus' relation to the Father. The competing term, favored by the Arians, was *homoiousios*, "similar essence," which was rejected by the Council. The Nicene Creed affirms that Jesus is fully divine. He is not just "similar to" God. He is God in the flesh, God incarnate!

> Q3. (Luke 1:35) What does the virgin conception teach us about Jesus' nature? How central is the doctrine of the virgin conception to the Christian message?
> http://www.joyfulheart.com/forums/index.php?showtopic=711

Nothing is Impossible with God (Luke 1:36-37)

After explaining that Mary's Child would be Holy and Divine, the angel lets Mary in on a family secret:

> "Even Elizabeth your relative is going to have a child in her old age, and she who was said to be

barren is in her sixth month. For nothing is impossible with God." (Luke 1:36-37)

Like Abraham's wife Sarah, Elizabeth, Mary's elderly relative was well beyond menopause. All her life she had been called barren, childless. That is until God wanted to do a miracle. And so Elizabeth's child John the Baptist was a "miracle baby," born to two senior citizens. The angel tells Mary: "Elizabeth, your cousin, is already six months pregnant, by the way."

And then he concludes, "For nothing is impossible with God!" Nothing.

Humanists and scientists for whom the scientific method is the only source of truth pooh-pooh the Virgin Birth as a myth. It couldn't happen! they scoff. It is true that post-menopausal women and virgins don't become pregnant – ever! But our experience of nature shouldn't tie God's hands. This is a miracle, by definition, "an extraordinary event manifesting divine intervention in human affairs."[13]

That's the angel's point. The Virgin Birth is impossible to man, but not to God. The angel's declaration to Mary is similar to such declarations throughout the Bible, beginning with the Angel of the Lord's announcement to Abraham that he would have a son when he was 99 and Sarah was 90:

- "Is anything too hard for the LORD?" (Genesis 18:14)

---

[13] *Merriam-Webster's 11th Collegiate Dictionary* (Merriam-Webster, 2003), p. 792.

- "Is the LORD's arm too short?" (Numbers 11:23)
- "Nothing is too hard for you." (Jeremiah 32:17, 27)
- "'Even though it seems impossible to the remnant of this people in these days, should it also seem impossible to me,' says the LORD of hosts?" (Zechariah 8:6, NRSV)
- "Jesus looked at them and said, 'With man this is impossible, but with God all things are possible.'" (Matthew 19:26 = Mark 10:27 = Luke 18:27)

Mary's Amazing Submission (Luke 1:38)

"'I am the Lord's servant,' Mary answered. 'May it be to me as you have said.' Then the angel left her." (Luke 1:38)

Every time I read Mary's response to the Angel's announcement and explanation, I am awed: "I am the Lord's servant. May it be to me as you have said." Here is a teenager facing misunderstanding and rejection from her family, her betrothed, and her townspeople. For a betrothed

Fra Angelico (Florentine painter, c. 1400-1455), "The Annunciation" (c. 1437), Fresco, Monastery of San Marco, Florence. Fresco, 230 x 321 cm.

woman to bear a child out of wedlock to someone not her husband could potentially even result in stoning (Deuteronomy 22:22-24). And yet she agrees. Mary affirms the bedrock truth that undergirds our discipleship: "I am the Lord's servant," or as the KJV puts it, "Behold, the handmaid of the Lord."

After all is said and done, after we have explored all the possibilities, we still must decide: am I a servant or a master? Is my allegiance to the Lord or to my own desires?

Sometimes it takes great turmoil in our souls to come to the place of submission, but come to it we must. Even before Jesus was conceived, Mary was faced with the decision: Will I obey and make way for this King? or Will I take the easy way that avoids difficulty and pain? To her everlasting credit, Mary's response of faith is what our response must be: "I am the Lord's servant. May it be to me as you have said."

Q4. (Luke 1:38) What is the essence of Mary's positive response to the angel? What can we learn from her response for our own lives? In what sense was Mary's response an "informed consent"? When we respond to God, what do we consent to?
http://www.joyfulheart.com/forums/index.php?showtopic=712

Blessed Mother of God (Luke 1:42-45)

Of course, Mary story doesn't end there, but begins. Soon after the angel's visit, Mary travels to visit her pregnant relative Elizabeth in the Judean hill country, several days journey south of Nazareth. When she arrives, Elizabeth's baby kicks hard, and Elizabeth speaks prophetically about Mary:

> "In a loud voice she exclaimed: 'Blessed are you among women, and blessed is the child you will bear! But why am I so favored, that the mother of my Lord should come to me? As soon as the sound of your greeting reached my ears, the baby in my womb leaped for joy. Blessed is she who has believed that what the Lord has said to her will be accomplished!'" (Luke 1:42-45)

I am including this prophecy because it give us greater insight into both Mary and her child. From the Angel's and Elizabeth's words come the "Hail Mary" prayer, *Ave Maria* in Latin. While the prayer itself dates from the Middle Ages, several elements derive directly from our passage.

"Hail Mary, full of grace, the Lord is with thee..."	"Hail, thou that art highly favored, the Lord is with thee..." (Luke 1:28, KJV)
"Blessed art thou among women, and blessed is the fruit of thy womb, Jesus."	"Blessed art thou among women, and blessed is the fruit of thy womb." (Luke 1:42, KJV)

| "Holy Mary, | "But why am I so favored, that |
| Mother of God...." | the mother of my Lord should come to me?" (Luke 1:43) |

I'm not suggesting praying to St. Mary herself or asking her to mediate or intercede for us with her Son as our mediatrix (1 Timothy 2:5). Jesus instructs his disciples of their privilege to pray directly to the Father in his name (John 16:26-27). Nevertheless, I am interested in how this prayer expresses much of what we know about Mary from Luke 1.

Two common titles for Mary derive from Elizabeth's prophetic insights:

"Blessed Virgin Mary" is a title commonly used by Catholic Christians. It comes directly from Elizabeth's exclamation: "Blessed art thou among women...." (1:42)

"Mother of God" may seem strange to Protestant ears, but it too derives from Elizabeth's description: "the mother of my Lord" (1:43). The *Ave Maria* substitutes the ancient phrase "Mother of God" (Greek *theotokos*). What an audacious statement! No one means by this, however, that somehow Mary preceded God as some kind of divine mother. Rather this is intended to express in clear terms that Mary in her womb was bearing the divine Son of God who is God himself, a union of both human and divine natures.[14]

---

[14] The use of the *theotokos*, "God-bearer" to describe Mary was part of the Nestorian controversy to define the union of human and divine natures

> Q5. (Luke 1:42-43) In what sense are the titles "Blessed Virgin Mary" and "Mother of God" appropriate for Mary? Why are we sometimes hesitant to exalt her as "blessed among women"?
> http://www.joyfulheart.com/forums/index.php?showtopic=713

Mary spends about three months with Elizabeth and was probably with her beloved, elderly kinswoman at the birth of John the Baptist. She is now perhaps four months pregnant herself and the life within her beginning to show. Now she must face her parents and her fiancé Joseph with the truth of this miracle that she cannot explain. But more of that when we study "Joseph, the Stand-In Father" in the next chapter.

In Mary we see an amazing young teenager who is entrusted by God to bear his Son and mother him through his growing-up years. Though she can't know all the future nor really understand, she

---

in one person, Christ. Just after the first Nicene Council, this controversy took place between Nestorius, Patriarch of Constantinople (who emphasized the distinction between Christ's human and divine natures) and his rival Cyril of Alexandria (who emphasized the union of Christ's natures). The discussion gets pretty obscure and theological, but it clarified the issues for the church. For more on this see J.N.D. Kelly, *Early Christian Doctrines* (Second Edition; Harper & Row, 1960), pp. 310-343.

responds, "I am the Lord's servant." No wonder the Church holds her in highest esteem to this day. May you and I be ready to respond with that same submitted willingness when God calls us to serve him.

Prayer

Lord, we are amazed at Mary's poise and composure through all this. We are awed by her humble submission. With the whole Church of Jesus, we honor Mary, the Blessed Virgin. Father, help me to count it an honor to be your servant, to be asked to serve you in a particular way. Help me to serve with joy and not with a grudging or complaining attitude. Help me to be a servant of whom you can be proud like your child Mary. In Jesus' name I pray. Amen.

Key Verses

> "'I am the Lord's servant,' Mary answered. 'May it be to me as you have said.'" (Luke 1:38)

> "Blessed are you among women, and blessed is the child you will bear! But why am I so favored, that the mother of my Lord should come to me?" (Luke 1:42-43)

2. Joseph, the Stand-In Father (Matthew 1:18-25)

The Gospel of Matthew begins with a detailed genealogy, beginning with Abraham, tracing through David, Israel's greatest king, and ending with:

> "Joseph, the husband of Mary, of whom was born Jesus, who is called Christ" (Matthew 1:16).

The genealogy traces Jesus' lineage back to David, placing him in line for the ultimate Kingship – Messiah, the anointed One, the heir to David's kingdom, who would rule over the Kingdom of God forever. But it's not that simple is it? Not nearly, since Jesus is born of a virgin mother, not of

Guido Reni, "St. Joseph with Infant Christ in his Arms" (1620s), oil on canvass 126x101 cm, Hermitage Museum, St. Petersburg.

Joseph's seed at all. Therefore, was Jesus really a descendent of David after all?

Matthew begins with a genealogy of the Messiah, of who begat whom, but now he must explain why it is relevant. This conception, this birth, bears some explanation.

It's pretty clear from what is *not* said in Matthew that his readers were familiar with the story of the virgin birth that Luke recounts, which had been told from Mary's point of view (Luke 1:26-38) and which we considered in a previous chapter. Matthew's account, on the other hand, is told from Joseph's perspective.

Matthew begins simply:

"This is how the birth of Jesus Christ came about: His mother Mary was pledged to be married to Joseph, but before they came together, she was found to be with child through the Holy Spirit." (Matthew 1:18)

Notice that he just states simply the facts of what his readers already knew, without embellishment:

1. Mary and Joseph were betrothed.[1]
2. They had not "come together," that is, had sex with each other.[2]

---

[1] "Pledged to be married" (NIV), "engaged" (NRSV), and "espoused" (KJV) translate the verb *mnēsteuō*, "woo and win, betroth," passive, "be betrothed, become engaged" (BDAG 656).

[2] "Came together" (NIV, KJV) or "lived together" (NRSV) is *synerchomai*, here "'to unite in an intimate relationship, come together' in a sexual context" (BDAG 969-970).

3. But Mary had begun to "show," she was pregnant.
4. The conception was from[3] the Holy Spirit, not man.

We knew these things and so did Joseph – except for point 4. In Matthew's account we learn how Joseph came to understand. The story is familiar to us, but let's examine it in detail so that we might begin to understand the stand-in father that the Heavenly Father chose to raise His Son.

Joseph's Name

Joseph's name was a proud name, recalling the ancient Jewish name of one of the twelve patriarchs, Joseph the son of Jacob who was sold by his brothers into Egypt and who later became second to Pharaoh in power over all Egypt, saving his family from famine (Genesis 30-50). His name means "to add."

Joseph the Husband

Joseph was no doubt older than Mary. While girls were married by 13 or 14 – old enough at that age to bear children – husbands on the other hand needed to be established enough to support a wife before they could enter into marriage. They were legally obligated to provide with food, clothing, and shelter.

---

[3] In 1:18 the Holy Spirit's agency is indicated by the preposition *ek*, here, a "marker denoting origin, cause, motive, reason, 'from, of.'" (BDAG 295-298, 3a).

But they didn't have to do it all by themselves. In the West, newly married couples get their own apartment and live independently, but not in Palestine. In first century Galilee, however, Joseph would take Mary home to the house in which he lived with his parents, and perhaps grandparents, as well as brothers and sisters who might be at home. Only as his own family grew, would Joseph and his family likely get their own house. This may sound very crowded and non-private to you, but it had its advantages. Instead of a young couple out on their

own, in a large household, each member contributed to the economy of the family by their own work, making enough for the whole to subsist on. A couple cut off from the economy of the extended family would have to fend for themselves, as Mary and Joseph had to do in Bethlehem. Those were mighty lean times.

Joseph the Carpenter

We know from later in Matthew's gospel that Joseph was a carpenter[4] by trade (Matthew 13:55). But the town of Nazareth was small enough that carpentry wouldn't have been all he did. Carpenters and other tradesmen would also keep a garden and a couple of animals for food and perhaps do some subsistence farming to eke out a living in this agrarian society of rural Galilee. But when townspeople needed some carpentry done that was

---

[4] Greek *tektōn*, "one who constructs, builder, carpenter" (BDAG 995).

2. Joseph, the Stand-In Father (Matthew 1:18-25)

beyond their own skills and tools, Joseph would be the one they came to.

As a rule the common man built his own house, probably with the help of family and neighbors. A family might have a knife and hammer of some kind. But a carpenter would possess both specialized tools, some fairly expensive, *and* the skills to use them – saws, axes, awls, drills, plumb lines, chisels, and planes, some of which have been recovered by archeologists.[5]

Georges de la Tour (French painter, 1593-1652), "Christ in the Carpenter's Shop" (1645), Oil on canvas, 137 x 101 cm, Musée du Louvre, Paris.

With these tools, a skilled carpenter might fashion doors, beams, and perhaps gates. He would make plows and yokes and other wood implements. There was no local Nazareth Furniture Store; all furniture would be made by hand. Each town had a rich family or two. They would be wanting some nice things made and their money would help the economy of the carpenter's family.

---

[5] R.K. Harrison, "Tools," ISBE 4:874-876.

But carpentry didn't make Joseph wealthy – not by any means. The offering Mary and Joseph brought to the temple on the occasion of Mary's purification from childbirth was the offering of a poor man, a pair of doves or pigeons (Luke 2:24; Leviticus 12:8).

Carpentry was Joseph's world, and the world that Jesus grew up in. He played in the wood shavings on the floor of his father's shop. Carpentry was Joseph's trade and the trade he taught his son. Jesus learned from Joseph to saw and plane, drill and smooth. He watched his father – the local contractor – make business contracts and deal with customers. Jesus saw it all.

> Q1. What would Jesus have learned as the son of a carpenter? What experiences would this have exposed him to?
> http://www.joyfulheart.com/forums/index.php?showtopic=714

Mary's Predicament, Joseph's Dilemma

But we're getting ahead of ourselves. Right now Joseph was faced with the pregnancy of his betrothed. You can bet that tongues in this small town were wagging furiously with the news. Mary is

2. Joseph, the Stand-In Father (Matthew 1:18-25)

pregnant! Couldn't Joseph and Mary wait? They know better!

Joseph has been deeply embarrassed by the whole incident. But he alone knows that he is *not* the father. He supposes that Mary, who as a betrothed woman and legally his wife, has had an affair with someone or another. Unless she had been raped, but she had said nothing of the sort! The only conclusion he can reach is that she has been unfaithful. His betrothed is an adulteress!

Mary's pregnancy had placed her at considerable risk in this society:

1. **Husband**. Her betrothed husband would reject her. Her pregnancy would embarrass him and reflect on his character. She couldn't expect him to understand or accept her condition.
2. **Penalty**. At worst she could be stoned. The law provided in cases like this for possible stoning (Deuteronomy 22:13-30), especially if the man and married woman are caught in the act of adultery. Stoning for adultery still took place in first century Palestine.[6]
3. **Shunning**. At best, her family would allow her to live at home, though her supposed

---

[6] Raymond E. Brown, *The Gospel According to John I-XII* (Anchor Bible; Doubleday, 1966), 333, citing J. Blinzer, "Die Strafe für Ehebruch in Bible and Halacha zur Auslegung von Joh. viii 5," NTS 4 (1957-58), 32-47.

adultery would hurt their standing in the community. She and her bastard child would be shunned.

4. **Remarriage**. No upstanding man would ever marry her, since the stigma of her supposed adultery would remain with her and taint the reputation of any husband.
5. **No where to go**. She couldn't go to the city and be lost in its anonymity. Single women just didn't live alone. This was a family-centered culture where a woman's work centered around home and family. There was no work for single women, except perhaps as a housekeeper in a wealthy home – or prostitution.

Mary's prospects were grim. She had agreed to the pregnancy. She had said to the angel, "Behold, I am the handmaid of the Lord. May it be to me according to your word" (Luke 1:38), but now the cost of this decision had become painfully apparent. However, the grace of God now comes into play.

Joseph, the Righteous Man (Matthew 1:19)

We begin to see the character of the man to whom she was betrothed:

> "Because Joseph her husband was a righteous man and did not want to expose her to public disgrace, he had in mind to divorce her quietly." (Matthew 1:19)

2. Joseph, the Stand-In Father (Matthew 1:18-25)

Matthew says that he was "a righteous man." "Righteous" (NIV, NRSV) or "just" (KJV) is *dikaios*, "pertaining to being in accordance with high standards of rectitude, upright, just, fair," here probably, "interested in doing the right thing, honorable, just, good."[7]

"Righteous" meant that Joseph carefully observed the law and valued his own reputation. According to the customs of that time, adultery would make her unmarriageable to either her betrothed husband or a paramour, if one had been discovered. By marrying her, Joseph would compromise himself in the eyes of the law. But his righteousness went deeper than a mere external righteousness before Jewish law. He was honorable and wanted to do the right thing.

Bartolomé Esteban Murillo (Spanish painter, 1617-1682), detail from "The Holy Family with a Small Bird" (c. 1650), Museo del Prado, Madrid.

The wrong thing, he decided, was to demand prosecuting her for adultery. "Expose to public

---

[7] *Dikaios*, BDAG 296-297, 1aα.

disgrace" (NIV, NRSV) or "make a public example" (KJV) is *deigmatizō*, "expose, make an example of, disgrace."[8] He couldn't marry her, of course, since he knew that her baby was not his. But instead of a messy public trial, he had decided to divorce[9] her quietly.[10] He would simply write out a certificate of divorce and present it to her in the presence of two witnesses, as required by law.[11] And to avoid the accusation of adultery as the reason for the divorce, Joseph could have offered less serious grounds, acknowledged by Pharisees of the school of Hillel. Brown suggests that "to divorce quietly" may mean to divorce *leniently*.[12]

And so Joseph decided to divorce Mary, but to do it in such a way as to protect her as much as he could, given the situation. We see in Joseph a gentleness and maturity. A righteous man, but not a man full of himself. Joseph was a man seeking to do the right thing.

---

[8] *Deigmatizō*, BDAG 214.
[9] "Divorce" (NIV), "dismiss" (NRSV), and "put away" (KJV) is *apoluō*, which is a technical term for "to grant acquittal, set free, release, pardon." Here it means, "to dissolve a marriage relationship, to divorce one's wife or betrothed" (BDAG 118, 5).
[10] "Quietly" (NIV) is *lathra*, "(to do something) without others being aware, secretly" (BDAG 581).
[11] Brown, *Birth*, p. 128, citing Strack and Billerback, I, 304-305.
[12] Brown, *Birth*, p. 128.

> Q2. (Matthew 1:19) What were Mary's options being pregnant and carrying a baby not her husband's? What kind of character did Joseph exhibit by deciding to divorce Mary quietly and leniently?
> http://www.joyfulheart.com/forums/index.php?showtopic=715

The Angel's Revelation in a Dream (Matthew 1:20-21)

God changed Joseph's mind:

> "But after he had considered this, an angel of the Lord appeared to him in a dream and said, 'Joseph son of David, do not be afraid to take Mary home as your wife, because what is conceived in her is from the Holy Spirit. She will give birth to a son, and you are to give him the name Jesus, because he will save his people from their sins.'" (Matthew 1:20-21)

The three times we have a record of God speaking to Joseph, it is through an "angel of the Lord" appearing to him in a dream. Each time when he wakes up, he immediately obeys the messenger (1:20; 2:13, 19). The form of address, "Son of David," emphasizes Joseph's honored position as a direct descendent of David, Israel's greatest king, and from whose descendents the Messiah should come.

The message was, "do not be afraid to take Mary home as your wife." Of course, according to Jewish law she was already his wife. But the messenger assures Joseph that it is right and just for him to proceed with the relationship.[13] Her pregnancy[14] is not adulterous, but "from the Holy Spirit."

The Name "Jesus" (Matthew 1:21)

Next, the angel tells Joseph the name to be given to the child – Jesus. "Jesus" (Greek *Iēsous*) was not an uncommon name at this time, since the Hebrew name *Yēshūa'* is a shortened form of Joshua (*Yehôshûa'*), who was one of Israel's most celebrated heroes. But the significance of God's insistence that he be named Jesus is not to honor a national hero, but because of the meaning of the name: "Yahweh saves."[15]

> "... You are to give him the name Jesus, because he will save his people from their sins" (Matthew 1:21)

Jesus' name from the time he was a baby was to indicate his mission. Both Mary and Joseph were given this name by the angel so neither would ever forget who he was – Yahweh's salvation embodied in human form. As a little baby, "Yahweh saves" might have been born and raised in the humblest of

---

[13] "Take home" (NIV) or "take" (NRSV, KJV) is *paralambanō*, "to take into close association, take (to oneself), take with/along." Here of one's wife, "take (her) into one's home," also 1:24. (BDAG 767).

[14] "Conceived" is *gennaō*, "beget" by procreation (BDAG 193-194).

[15] The original meaning is "Yahweh helps," or in popular etymology connected with the root *ysh'*, "to save," and the noun *yeshû'â*, "salvation" (Brown, *Birth*, p. 131).

circumstances, but that never diminished who he was. His destiny was to save. The Greek verb *sōzō* means "to preserve or rescue from natural dangers and afflictions, save, keep from harm, preserve, rescue," here, "to save/preserve from eternal death, bring Messianic salvation."[16]

Seeing the Messiah as Savior was the popular Jewish understanding of the Messiah's role at the time. But the angel made it clear to Joseph that this salvation would not be political or military. Jesus' mission was not to overthrow the Roman oppressors and reinstate the Jewish kingdom. His mission was to save his people from a far more insidious enemy – sin. Jesus came to destroy the power of sin.

Q3. (Matthew 1:21) What is the significance of the name Jesus? Why do you think the angel gave the name to both Mary (Luke 1:31) and Joseph independently?
http://www.joyfulheart.com/forums/index.php?showtopic=716

---

[16] *Sōzō*, BDAG 982-983.

Joseph Shall Adopt the Child (Matthew 1:21)

Before we leave it, let's take one final look at this command:

"... You are to give him the name Jesus" (Matthew 1:21)

Joseph is commanded to personally name[17] the child. This is deeply significant. It means that Joseph, in naming the child, acknowledges him as his own son and thus becomes the legal father of the child according to Semitic law. As a result of this legal adoption, Joseph's ancestry as a descendent of David transfers also to his legal son.[18] Biologically, Jesus is begotten by the Holy Spirit and is thus the "Son of God" (Luke 1:32a), but legally he is the son of Joseph and heir to the promises of David, Joseph's ancestor.

The angel Gabriel had promised Mary, "The Lord God will give him the throne of his father David" (Luke 1:32b). In Joseph naming the boy, and therefore adopting him, David becomes Jesus' earthly ancestor.

The Virgin Will Conceive (Matthew 1:22-23)

The angel's message is complete. Now Matthew explains all this in terms of an ancient prophetic word:

---

[17] The verb is *kaleō*, "call," here with the meaning "name, provide with a name" (BDAG 502-504, 1c.).

[18] See the discussion in Brown, *Birth*, p. 139.

2. Joseph, the Stand-In Father (Matthew 1:18-25)

"All this took place to fulfill what the Lord had said through the prophet: The virgin will be with child and will give birth to a son, and they will call him Immanuel' – which means, 'God with us.'" (Matthew 1:22-23)

Matthew is quoting Isaiah 7:14 because he sees in it a prefiguring of the Virgin Birth of Jesus.

In its original setting, Isaiah is exhorting Ahaz King of Judah (the southern kingdom), who faces the daunting threat of a siege of Jerusalem by the armies of Israel (the northern kingdom) and its ally Aram-Damascus, a petty Syrian kingdom. Isaiah tells Ahaz not to fear, but to stand firm in faith. As a sign, the Lord says that a virgin will conceive and bear a child to be called Immanuel as a reminder that God is with his people in times of trouble. In the time it will take this baby to become just a young child, the King of Assyria will have destroyed Judah's enemies.

Some believe that the reference is to some child born in Isaiah's day.[19] Others see in it a brief prophetic insight, a glimpse far into the future of a child who will be born to a virgin and bring God's very presence to deliver his people.[20] Clearly, Matthew

---

[19] John N. Oswalt, *The Book of Isaiah, Chapters 1-39* (New International Commentary on the Old Testament; Eerdmans, 1986), p. 209-213. Oswalt sees Isaiah's son Maher-shalal-hash-baz (Isaiah 8:3) as the immediate fulfillment, but with 7:14 pointing to "the ultimate Immanuel" (p. 213).

[20] For example, Edward J. Young, *The Book of Isaiah* (Eerdmans, 1965), vol. 1, pp. 283-294. He quotes the classic work of J. Gresham Machen, *The Virgin Birth of Christ* (1930), who paraphrases the thought: "I see a wonderful child, the prophet on this interpretation would say, a wonderful child whose birth shall bring salvation to his people; and

sees the virgin conception and the name Immanuel as having a fuller meaning in Christ. The word "fulfill" (*plēroō*) means "to make full, fill(full)," then "to bring to completion, complete, finish" and as here "to bring to a designed end, fulfill" a prophecy.[21]

Prophecy in the Old Testament takes several shapes, including:

1. **Exhortation**, a directive word from God to a particular person or people at a particular time. For example, the Prophet Nathan confronts David with his adultery: "Thou art the man!" (2 Samuel 12).
2. **Prediction**, a clear foretelling of the future for a person or nation. For example, the Prophet Isaiah foresees the Suffering Servant in Isaiah 53 and declares his atonement for our sins.
3. **Acted prophecy**, such as Hosea marrying a prostitute to illustrate Israel's unfaithfulness (Hosea 1:2).
4. **Foreshadowing**, where a contemporary prophetic event or insight foreshadows a distant one, so there is a double fulfillment – a present-time fulfillment (the type) and a fu-

---

before such a period of time shall elapse as would lie between the conception of the child in his mother's womb and his coming to years of discretion, the land of Israel and of Syria shall be forsaken." Young comments, "In vision Isaiah was allowed to see the virgin, and it is the announcement of what he is permitted to see in vision that he declared unto Ahaz and the nation" (p. 286).

[21] *Plēroō*, BDAG 827-829, 4a.

ture completion (the antitype) which brings the prophecy to fullness or completion.

I see Isaiah's words in Isaiah 7:14 as the latter kind of prophetic word. The initial fulfillment presumably took place in the prophet's time, while the ultimate fulfillment and completion of this word is found in Christ.

> Q4. (Matthew 1:23) How did the prophetic concept of the virgin conception and the name "Immanuel" find their fullness in the birth of Jesus to Mary?
> http://www.joyfulheart.com/forums/index.php?showtopic=717

Emmanuel, God with Us (Matthew 1:23)

"Emmanuel" or "Immanuel" (depending upon how one spells it) is a transliteration of the Hebrew name in Isaiah 7:14, literally "with us is God,"[22] originally symbolizing the presence of God (*'el*) to deliver his people from the Assyrian army that threatened their very existence in Isaiah's day. Though to our knowledge, the name Immanuel was never given to Jesus, it certainly applied to him, since "God with us" is a perfect way to describe the birth of

---

[22] BDB 769.

Joseph's Obedience (Matthew 1:24-25)

> "When Joseph woke up, he did what the angel of the Lord had commanded him and took Mary home as his wife. But he had no union with her until she gave birth to a son. And he gave him the name Jesus." (Matthew 1:24-25)

As soon as he woke up,[23] Joseph obeyed. He accepted Mary as his wife, and took her home, but didn't have sex[24] with her until Jesus was born.

Did he have normal marital relations with her *after* Jesus' birth? Protestants see verse 25 as evidence that Mary and Joseph lived together as husband and wife after Jesus' birth and bore additional children together, since there is no suggestion that Jesus' brothers and sisters (Matthew 12:46-50; 13:55-56) were not also children of Mary and Joseph. While the Greek conjunction *heōs*, "until" doesn't *demand* that they later had marital relations, that is certainly the implication.[25] Catholics, on the other hand, believe

---

[23] "Woke up" (NIV) or literally "being raised" (KJV), is the Aorist passive of *egeirō*, "wake, arouse," or passive, "wake up, awaken." (BDAG 271-272, 1, 2.). The word also is used in a command to the dreaming Joseph in Matthew 2:13.

[24] "Had no union" (NIV), "had no marital relations" (NRSV) or "knew" (KJV) is *ginōskō*, "know," here a euphemism for "to have sexual intercourse with," both here and in Luke 1:34 (BDAG 199-200, 5).

[25] "Until" is *heōs*, "to denote the end of a period of time, till, until." 1.b.β, Aleph). It is used both here and in 2:15 where it refers to the period of time that the Holy Family lived as expatriates in Egypt. Catholic New Testament scholar Raymond E. Brown (*Birth*, p. 132), in

that these children were Joseph's by a previous marriage and that the Virgin Mary was a perpetual virgin.

> Q5. (1:24-25) What does Joseph accepting Mary as his wife say about his character? What is the significance for prophetic fulfillment of Jesus as a Son of David that Joseph "named" the child "Jesus"?
> http://www.joyfulheart.com/forums/index.php?showtopic=718

Joseph Protects Jesus (Matthew 2:13-15)

The final things we learn about Joseph happen a few years after Jesus' birth, but let's consider them briefly. First, after the wise men came to worship

---

protecting the doctrine of the Perpetual Virginity of Mary, notes that in English when something is negated *until* a particular time, something happening *after* that time is usually assumed. However, he cites K. Beyer (*Semitische Syntax im Neuen Testament* (Göttigen: Vandenhoeck, 1962), I, 132) to the effect that in Greek and Semitic such a negation often has no implication about what happened afterwards. Note this argument only provides the *possibility* that *heōs* ("until") doesn't imply that Mary and Joseph engaged in marital relations later; it doesn't prove the point. Although Brown asserts, "The immediate context favors a lack of future implication here," in the light of Matthew 12:46-50; 13:55-56, I don't agree. If Matthew had intended to teach Mary's perpetual virginity, he would have said something like, "Though Joseph took Mary home as his wife, he never had sex with her." Instead, he uses *heōs* ("until") with a specified time period, "until she gave birth to a son." Brown concludes, "In my judgment the question of Mary's remaining a virgin for the rest of her life belongs to post-biblical theology."

Jesus – and had tipped off King Herod as to the presence of a possible rival heir to the throne – an angel commanded Joseph to flee (Matthew 2:13-15). Joseph obeyed immediately and left in the middle of the night for Egypt. It was a good thing he did. Within a short time, Herod's soldiers slaughtered all the male babies in Bethlehem.

After Herod's death – when he perceived that the threat was over –Joseph brought Mary and the Child back to Israel, returning to Nazareth (2:19-23). Even then, he is careful not to return to Bethlehem, since Herod's brutal son Archelaus now reigned in the territory of Judah.[26] So he brought his family back to Nazareth, in spite of what scandal still might remain there. In Nazareth, the family now lived. It was here that Jesus was raised, and learned the trade of carpentry from his father.

The scripture tells us nothing of Joseph's death, though presumably he was not living during the time of Jesus' ministry, or Jesus would not have felt the need to entrust his mother Mary's care to the beloved disciple (John 19:26-27).

---

[26] Herod the Great's death is probably to be dated as March/April 4 B.C. (Brown, *Birth*, p. 166.) Succeeded in Judea by his son Archelaus who was technically an ethnarch in Judea. He was known for his brutality and dictatorial ways, so much so that the Jews sent a deputation to Rome seeking his removal. He was deposed by Rome in 6 AD But Joseph could take no chances with a ruler with such a savage reputation. Joseph was a known and marked man. If someone recognized him in Bethlehem, the child might well have been killed by the son Archelaus. So instead Joseph led his family to Nazareth. In spite of the scandal of Mary's pregnancy there, he would not be identified with the wisemen's visit to Bethlehem. The Child would be safe.

What we learn from the Scripture about Joseph is that God chose to father his Jesus a man who was devout, full of faith, obedient to God, just, merciful, and one who loved and carefully guarded both Mary and the Child Jesus.

Prayer

Father, thank you for Joseph who proved worthy of your trust to raise Jesus. Help us to be as believing, as faithful, as zealous as he was to take on the various tasks that you assign to us. In Jesus' name, we pray. Amen.

Key Verses

> "Because Joseph her husband was a righteous man and did not want to expose her to public disgrace, he had in mind to divorce her quietly." (Matthew 1:19)

> "When Joseph woke up, he did what the angel of the Lord had commanded him and took Mary home as his wife." (Matthew 1:24)

3. The Shepherds' Sign of the Manger (Luke 2:1-20)

How cute to see some girl's doll, recruited at the last minute and wrapped tightly in a blanket, lying amidst the straw of an X-ended manger that dwells the remainder of the year in the church attic.

Gerard (Gerrit) van Honthorst (1590–1656), Adoration of the Shepherds (1622). 164 x 190 cm, Wallraf-Richartz-Museum, Cologne.

Jessica stands in for Mary, while Robert, the tallest boy in Sunday school this year, makes a perfect Joseph – once they've applied his fake beard.

Now don't get me wrong. I'm not at all against nativity scenes. But we've seen so many, year after year, that it's hard for us to read Scripture and see with fresh eyes what it actually says to us. Luke 2:1-7 makes four important points about the birth of Jesus:

3. The Shepherds' Sign of the Manger (Luke 2:1-20)

1. Jesus is born in history.
2. Jesus is born in David's birthplace.
3. Jesus' birth is attended by hardship.
4. Jesus is born in humble circumstances.

1. Jesus Is Born in History (Luke 2:1-2)

"In those days Caesar Augustus issued a decree that a census should be taken of the entire Roman world. (This was the first census that took place while Quirinius was governor of Syria.)" (Luke 2:1-2)

Jesus has an historical context; he's neither a myth nor a legend. He is both historical and verifiable. He is mentioned not only in the New Testament, but by contemporaries and early documents such as Josephus, Pliny, Tacitus, Suetonius, Bar-Serapion, Thallus, Lucian, and the Talmud.[1] Jesus is a person in history.

Jesus' historical setting includes rulers Caesar Augustus, Herod the Great, and Quirinius. "Caesar Augustus," Roman emperor Octavian, reigned 27 BC - 14 AD. Herod the Great, called "King of the Jews," ruled Judea from 40 to 4 BC. Quirinius was a military leader and Roman consul in central Asia Minor, and later Imperial Legate of Syria-Cilicia (AD 6 to 9), where Josephus notes that he conducted a census.[2] The census in our passage isn't recorded elsewhere

---

[1] Josh McDowell, *Evidence That Demands a Verdict* (Campus Crusade for Christ, 1972), documents all these references and more in Chapter 5: "Jesus–a Man of History," pp. 83-89.

[2] Josephus, *Antiquities* 18.1-3,26, referred to in Acts 5:37.

but makes sense, perhaps under a kind of extraordinary command authority Quirinius possessed during his military maneuvers in Cilicia or during a brief earlier stint as governor in Syria.[3]

> Q1. (Luke 2:1-2) Why does Luke name the rulers in 2:1-2? What point is he making?
> http://www.joyfulheart.com/forums/index.php?showtopic=719

2. Jesus Is Born in David's Birthplace (Luke 2:3-4)

> "And everyone went to his own town to register. So Joseph also went up from the town of Nazareth in Galilee to Judea, to Bethlehem the town of David, because he belonged to the house and line of David." (Luke 2:3-4)

The second point of our passage is that Jesus was born in the birthplace of David, Israel's greatest King. Nearly 1000 years before Jesus' birth, God had promised to David through the Prophet Samuel,

---

[3] The controversy surrounding Quirinius and this census are discussed fully in Craig L. Blomberg, "Quirinius," ISBE 3:12-13; and Marshall, *Luke*, pp. 99-105. Usually Romans conducted a census where residents lived, but there is a precedent for the procedure we see in Luke 2:3-5. A decree of C. Vibius Maximus, dated in AD 104, required absentees to return to their home towns for a census in Egypt (P. Lond. 904, 20f; cited in J.M. Creed, *St. Luke*, London: Macmillan, 1930).

3. The Shepherds' Sign of the Manger (Luke 2:1-20)

"Your house and your kingdom will endure forever before me; your throne will be established forever" (2 Samuel 7:16).

Micah had also prophesied of Bethlehem as the birthplace of the Messiah (Micah 5:2)

The Jews eagerly expected David's successor and called this hoped-for Messiah the "Son of David." Jesus is the Son of David, this promised King. It is no accident that Joseph was "of the house and lineage of David" (Luke 2:4, KJV) and that Jesus was born in Bethlehem.[4]

---

[4] A phrase in John Hopkins Jr.'s carol "We Three Kings" (1857) got me wondering: "Born a king on Bethlehem's plain." How could a town in the "hill country of Judah" have a plain? Bethlehem sits near the crest of the Judean central mountain spine that runs north and south in Israel, west of the Great Rift Valley and east of the coastal plains that taper down to the Mediterranean to the west. A look at Google Earth or Google Maps makes clear its mountainous topography, as do photos of the town. Yet we see general reference to a plain in "Joy to the World" ("rocks, hills, and plains"), Isaac Watts (1719). But the references to a plain in Bethlehem where shepherds watched sheep is especially clear among nineteenth century song writers: "It Came Upon a Midnight Clear" ("above its sad and lowly plains..."), Edmund H. Sears (1849); "Shepherds Watching O'er the Plain," Mrs. Gaskell (1916); "The Shepherds on Fair Bethlehem's Plain," Edward G. Selden (1916), "Blessèd Night, When First that Plain," Horatius Bonar (1857); "When, Marshaled on the Nightly Plain," Henry K. White (1812); "Far, Far Away on Judea's Plains," John M. Macfarlane (1869); and "On Judah's Plains as Shepherds Sat," unknown author (1849). Even Edersheim's editor in *Life and Times of Jesus the Messiah* (1887) makes that mistake (1:187). I guess in their romanticizing of the birth of Christ, song writers in the nineteenth century never traveled to the Holy Land.

3. Jesus' Birth Is Attended by Hardship (Luke 2:5-6)

"He went there to register with Mary, who was pledged to be married to him and was expecting a child. While they were there, the time came for the baby to be born." (Luke 2:5-6)

The most glorious event in history is about to unfold, but for Joseph and Mary it is drudgery and hardship.

- Mary and Joseph live in Nazareth, four days journey north of Bethlehem.
- Mary is pregnant. A journey late in pregnancy is arduous for her. But if she stays in Nazareth she has to face scandal alone. Luke puts it delicately: "... Mary, who was pledged to be married to him and was expecting a child" (2:5).
- Compounding that, it could well have been winter, if second century church tradition is to be taken seriously.[5]

An arduous journey in winter, a pregnant teenage mom. Who says that following God's plan is easy? Just because we face hardships and obstacles is no

---

[5] The date of December 25 goes back to Hippolytus (AD 165-235), and Chrysostom (AD 345-407), who stated in 386 that December 25 is the correct day. Brief discussion in William P. Armstrong and Jack Finegan, "Chronology of the New Testament," ISBE 1:688.

indication that God is absent, that we've missed his will.

> Q2. Why do you think the journey to Bethlehem was difficult for Mary? Is pleasure an indication that we are in God's will or not? Any examples from your life? Extra Credit: Argue for or against this proposition: "Being a consistent Christian causes more hardships than just going with the flow."
> http://www.joyfulheart.com/forums/index.php?showtopic=720

4. Jesus Is Born in Humble Circumstances (Luke 2:7)

> "... And she gave birth to her firstborn, a son. She wrapped him in cloths and placed him in a manger, because there was no room for them in the inn." (Luke 2:7)

The manger astounds me. The holy Son of God was born in a stable or cave where animals were kept and his first crib was a common cattle trough. Why? Though Jesus was by very nature God (Philippians 2:6), he didn't grasp at his prerogatives or flaunt his rights. Instead, he

"Made himself nothing (*kenoō*),
taking the very nature of a servant,
being made in human likeness...." (Philippians 2:7)

Kenoō means "make empty."[6] Jesus literally "emptied himself" of all the privileges to which he was heir. He didn't just take a low place, he took the lowest place. His commission was "to preach good news to the poor" (Luke 4:18; quoting Isaiah 61:1), so he was born among the poorest of the poor. His disciples argued about who would be greatest in the Kingdom, but Jesus stopped them short:

> "For even the Son of Man did not come to be served, but to serve, and to give his life as a ransom for many." (Mark 10:45)

The manger represents serving.

Shepherds Keeping Watch over Their Flocks (Luke 2:8)

But the manger was more than a symbol of humility. God planned it as a sign. Let's read on.

> "And there were shepherds living out in the fields nearby, keeping watch over their flocks at night." (Luke 2:8)

Sheep raised on the hillsides around Bethlehem may well have been destined for temple sacrifices in Jerusalem, only six miles to the north.[7] Jeremias describes a shepherd's life:

---

[6] *Kenoō*, BDAG 539, 1b.

[7] Morris, *Luke*, p. 84. He cites Rabbinical sources that flocks were only to be kept in the wilderness (*Mishnah, Baba Kamma* 7:7; *Talmud, Baba*

3. The Shepherds' Sign of the Manger (Luke 2:1-20)

"The dryness of the ground made it necessary for the flocks of sheep and cattle to move about during the rainless summer and to stay for months at a time in isolated areas, far from the owner's home. Hence, herding sheep was an independent and responsible job; indeed, in view of the threat of wild beasts and robbers, it could even be dangerous. Sometimes the owner himself (Luke 15:6; John 10:12) or his sons did the job. But usually it was done by hired shepherds, who only too often did not justify the confidence reposed in them (John 10:12-13)."[8]

Some of Israel's great heroes were shepherds – Abraham, Isaac, Jacob, and David. But in the First Century, it seems, shepherds – specifically, hireling shepherds – had a rather unsavory reputation. The Rabbis are quoted as saying, "most of the time they were dishonest and thieving; they led their herds onto other people's land and pilfered the produce of the land." Because they were often months at a time without supervision, they were often accused of stealing some of the increase of the flock. Consequently, the pious were warned not to buy wool, milk, or kids from shepherds on the assumption that it was stolen property.[9] Shepherds were not allowed

---

Kamma 79b-80a). Any animal found between Jerusalem and a spot near Bethlehem must be presumed to be a sacrificial victim (Mishnah, *Shekalim* 7:4).

[8] Joachim Jeremias, *poimēn, ktl.*, TDNT 6:485-502.

[9] Joachim Jeremias, *Jerusalem in the Time of Jesus* (SCM/Fortress Press, 1969), pp. 304-305. He cites *b. Sanh.* 25b; Strack and Billerback II, 114; *M.B.K.* x.9; *T.B.K.* xi.9, 370; *b. Ket.* 62b; *b.B.K.* 94b *Bar*. Green, *Luke*, p. 130, disputes this analysis. Rather, he sees them merely as "peasants, located

to fulfill a judicial office or be admitted in court as witnesses.[10] A midrash on Psalm 23:2 reads, "There is no more disreputable occupation than that of a shepherd."[11] Philo, a Hellenistic Jewish philosopher of Alexandria (25 BC - 45 AD), wrote about looking after sheep and goats, "Such pursuits are held mean and inglorious."[12]

They lived outside most of the year. "Abiding in the field" (KJV) is the Greek verb *agrauleō*, "live out of doors."[13] Flocks were kept outside in this way from April to November, and, sometimes during the winter in suitable locations.[14] Shepherds were constantly with their sheep, since the sheep were vulnerable to all kinds of trouble. "Keeping watch" is a combination of two related Greek words, *phylassō*, "to carry out sentinel functions, watch, guard,"[15] and *phylakē*, "the act of guarding." Together they carry the idea of "keep watch, do guard duty."[16] The shepherds made sure that the sheep were safe from wandering off and injuring themselves, as well as dangers from thieves and wolves.

---

toward the bottom of the scale of power and privilege." Marshall, *Luke*, p. 108, too, notes that the tradition of despised shepherds is late.

[10] Jeremias, *poimne, ktl.*, TDNT 6:489.
[11] *Midrash* Ps. 23.2, ed. Buber, Vilna 1891, 99b.12, cited by Jeremias, *Jerusalem*, p. 311, fn. 42.
[12] Philo, *de agric.* 61, cited by Jeremias, *Jerusalem*, p. 311, fn. 42.
[13] *Agrauleō*, BDAG 15.
[14] Marshall, *Luke*, p. 108, cites Strack and Billerback II, 114-116; Morris, *Luke*, p. 84.
[15] *Phylassō*, BDAG 1068.
[16] *Phylakē*, BDAG 1067.

The Glory of the Lord (Luke 2:9)

One minute the shepherds are talking quietly in the blackness of the winter sky. The next moment the hillside is ablaze with light and booming with the sound of an angel's voice.

> "An angel of the Lord appeared to them, and the glory of the Lord shone around them, and they were terrified." (2:9)

The brightness is more than just mega-candlepower. It is the radiance of God's own glory. "Glory" (*doxa*, which we also see in verse 14) refers to "the condition of being bright or shining, brightness, splendor, radiance."[17] Throughout the Old Testament the presence of God is referred to as overwhelmingly bright, burning as fire, such as the cloud above the tabernacle by day and the pillar of fire by night.[18] God's angels sometimes bear this same bright glory (Matthew 28:3; Luke 24:4; Daniel 10:6). In this case the glory shines around the whole area. The shepherds are frozen in terror. "Terrified" (NIV) or "sore afraid" (KJV) reads, literally, "feared with a great fear."

---

[17] *Doxa*, BDAG 257.
[18] Exodus 16:7, 10; 40:34-35; 1 Kings 8:11; Isaiah 6:3; 40:5; 60:1; Ezekiel 3:23; 2 Corinthians 3:18; 4:4; etc.

> Q3. (Luke 2:7-8) Why do you think the message of Jesus' birth comes to shepherds, of all people? Why is Jesus born in a stable with a manger for a bed? This has to be intentional. What point is God making?
> http://www.joyfulheart.com/forums/index.php?showtopic=721

The Good News Angel (Luke 2:10-11)

The angel moves first to calm their fears....

> "But the angel said to them, 'Do not be afraid. I bring you good news of great joy that will be for all the people. Today in the town of David a Savior has been born to you; he is Christ the Lord.'" (Luke 2:10-11)

This Good News angel has the enviable task of being the first herald of Messiah's birth. "Bring good news" (NIV) or "bring good tidings" (KJV) is the Greek verb *euangelizō*, from which we get our English word, "evangelize." Here it means, "bring good news, announce good news." Later in the New Testament it is widely used for "proclaim the message of salvation, preach the gospel."[1] This is

---

[1] *Euangelizō*, BDAG 402.

very good news that results in joy,[2] intensified by the Greek adjective *megas*, "great, above standard in intensity."[3] This is great joy indeed!

Notice how broad is the angel's message. It is not for just the pious or for the Jew, but "for all the people." What wonderful news for those who are estranged from God and struggling under oppression! The baby is not just born to Mary and Joseph. The baby is born "to you" – to the shepherd recipients of the message and all others.

"The town of David"[4] reminds the reader of the Messiah-child's connection with his ancestor David. Prophecy indicates that the Messiah will be born in Bethlehem. And what a fitting prophecy for these Bethlehem shepherds to recall, given 730 years previously by the prophet Micah:

> "But you, Bethlehem Ephrathah,
> though you are small among the clans of Judah,
> out of you will come for me
> one who will be ruler over Israel,
> whose origins are from of old,
> from ancient times....
>
> He will stand and shepherd his flock
> in the strength of the Lord,
> in the majesty of the name of the Lord his God.
> And they will live securely, for then his greatness

---

[2] *Chara*, "the experience of gladness, joy" (BDAG 1077).
[3] *Megas*, BDAG 623-624.
[4] "City" or "town" is the Greek noun *polis*, which can refer "a population center of varying size," BDAG 844-845.

will reach to the ends of the earth.
And he will be their peace." (Micah 5:2-3, 5a)

A Savior (Luke 2:11)

The angel also calls this baby "Savior" (*sōtēr*) "one who rescues, savior, deliverer, preserver."[5] In the prophecies about Jesus' birth in Luke 1-3 we observe this theme several times (1:69, 17, 77; 2:30-32; 3:6 from Isaiah 40:5). Jesus, quoting Isaiah, spelled out his mission this way:

> "The Spirit of the Lord is on me,
> because he has anointed me
> to preach good news to the poor.
> He has sent me to proclaim
> freedom for the prisoners
> and recovery of sight for the blind,
> to release the oppressed,
> to proclaim the year of the Lord's favor."
> (Luke 4:18-19, quoting from Isaiah 61:1-2)

This Savior will bring both salvation from enemies and from sin – but not just to the Jews but also to the Gentiles – all people!

Christ the Lord (Luke 2:11)

Finally, the angel utters the words that Jews had longed for centuries to hear – "He is Christ the Lord." Messiah! This Child is Messiah!

Our English word "Christ," of course, comes from the Greek adjective *christos*, "anointed," which

---

[5] *Sōtēr*, BDAG 985.

translates Hebrew *mashiah*, transliterated in English as "messiah."[6] The angel's declaration, however, doesn't use the word "Christ" by itself, but in the phrase, "Christ the Lord." "Lord" (*kyrios*) means "owner, lord, master, a designation of any person of high position."[7] Jews were used to reading "Lord" whenever the divine name "Yahweh" appeared in Scripture, so to Jewish ears, these two words, *christos* and *kyrios* spoke of divinity. The meaning seems to "the highest conceivable and most lofty designation of Christ,"[8] that is, "The Lord Messiah" or "the Messiah (and) the Lord" with connotations of *kyrios* used of Yahweh himself, rather than just of an exalted personage – a Savior who can be regarded as the Messiah-Yahweh.[9] The implications of this exalted title are staggering!

Q4. (Luke 2:11) What are the three titles of Jesus given by the angels? What does each mean? What does this tell us about Jesus' true identity?
http://www.joyfulheart.com/forums/index.php?showtopic=722

---

[6] See notes on *mashiah*, TWOT #1255c.
[7] *Kyrios*, BDAG 576-579.
[8] Walter Grundmann, *chrio, ktl.*, TDNT 9:532-33, quoting H. Sahlin.
[9] Marshall, *Luke*, p. 110. Cf. Green, *Luke*, p. 135.

At the Sign of a Manger (Luke 2:12)

The shepherds are given a sign that the angel's message is true:

> "This will be a sign to you: You will find a baby wrapped in cloths and lying in a manger." (Luke 2:12)

"Sign" (*sēmeion*) means "a sign or distinguishing mark whereby something is known, sign, token, indication."[10] The sign consists of two elements. The baby is: (1) wrapped in cloths, and (2) lying in a manger.

The phrase "wrapped in swaddling clothes" (KJV) or "cloths" (NIV) translates the Greek verb *sparganoō*, "to wrap in pieces of cloth used for swaddling infants, wrap up in cloths."[11] These were "strips of cloth like bandages, wrapped around young infants in order "to keep their limbs straight."[12] This was pretty common.

However, the second sign was that the newborn would be found in a *manger* – that *was* unique! The Greek noun is *phatnē*, "manger, crib, feeding-trough."[13] A manager would indicate the location in

---

[10] *Sēmeion*, BDAG 920.

[11] *Sparganoō*, BDAG 936. We don't use the English word "swaddle" much anymore, but it is derived from the Old English word *swathain*, "to swathe, bind, wrap."

[12] Marshall, *Luke*, p. 106, cites Ezekiel 16:4 and Wisdom 7:4.

[13] *Phatnē*, BDAG 1050. The lexicographer indicates that the term "could perhaps be a stable or even a feeding-place under the open sky, in contrast to *katalyma*, a shelter where people stayed." The predominant idea of this word group is of feeding animals. Martin Hengel, *phatnē*,

some kind of stable. A second century legend indicates that this was in a cave.[14]

Glory to God in the Highest (Luke 2:13-14)

After the angel's startling declaration, the heavens reveal a huge crowd of angelic beings:

> "Suddenly a great company of the heavenly host appeared with the angel, praising God and saying,
> 'Glory to God in the highest,
> and on earth peace to men
> on whom his favor rests.'" (Luke 2:13-14)

The crowd is described with two phrases: (1) "great company" or "multitude"[15] and (2) "heavenly host." "Host" is the Greek noun *strateia*, a military term that means "army."[16] God's heavenly army is mentioned several times in scripture.[17]

This heavenly army is praising God.[18] It may have been a heavenly choir as in popular Christmas lore, but the scripture doesn't explicitly say that they are singing as the angels in Revelation (5:11-13; 15:3). Here they seem to be chanting in unison or speaking (Greek *legō*, "utter words, say").

TDNT 9:49-55, denies the possibility in our context that this can be translated "stall."

[14] Ibid. Also Joachim Jeremias, *poimēn, ktl.*, TDNT 6:491, fn. 59. A cave in Bethlehem was honored by Christians as Christ's birthplace as early as the early second century AD.

[15] *Plēthos*, "crowd, throng, host, assembly" (BDAG 825-826).

[16] Otto Bauernfeind, *strateuomai ktl.*, TDNT 7:701-713.

[17] Joshua 5:14; 2 Kings 6:17; Psalm 34:7; 103:21; 148:2.

[18] *Aineō*, here and in verse 20, means "to praise," with the root idea of "express approval" (BDAG 27).

The content of their praise is (1) to give glory to God and (2) to offer a blessing of peace to men. "Glory" (*doxa*) is used here in the sense of "honor as an enhancement or recognition of status or performance, fame, recognition, renown, honor, prestige."[19] The angels promise peace (Greek *eirēnē*) – peace between God and mankind, which essentially amounts to salvation.

We're used to the wording: "on earth peace, good will toward men," (KJV) but more ancient Greek manuscripts indicate a better translation: "on earth peace to men on whom his favor rests" (NIV).[20] The idea is that God extends his peace and salvation to his favored people, those whom he sovereignly chooses or elects to favor and save.

The Shepherd's Response (Luke 2:15-18)

Now the shepherds have a choice.

---

[19] "Glory" is often used in the New Testament in the context of praise: Luke 19:38; Ephesians 1:6; 3:21; Philippians 2:11; Revelation 5:13 (BDAG 257-258). These angels honor God as being highest (Greek *hypsistos*) in a spatial sense, in contrast to earth (mentioned in the next phrase) (BDAG 1045). Also Georg Bertram, *hypsistos*, TDNT 8:619.

[20] The meaning of this phrase depends upon the case (nominative or genitive) of *eudokia*, which can mean either, (1) "state or condition of being kindly disposed, good will," or (2) "state or condition of being favored, favor, good pleasure" (BDAG 404-405). The KJV translation based on the Textus Receptus renders "good will" (*eudokia*) in the nominative case. However, newer translations, based on the oldest Alexandrian and Western Greek manuscripts, render it in the genitive case, "on earth peace among those whom he favors" (NRSV). Similar Semitic phrases – "sons of his [God's] good pleasure" and "the elect of his good pleasure" – occur in several Qumran hymns. (Bruce M. Metzger, *A Textual Commentary on the Greek New Testament* (United Bible Societies, 1971), p. 133, citing *1 QH* iv.32f.; xi.9; viii.6. Marshall, p. 112).

> "When the angels had left them and gone into heaven, the shepherds said to one another, 'Let's go to Bethlehem and see this thing that has happened, which the Lord has told us about.' So they hurried off and found Mary and Joseph, and the baby, who was lying in the manger. When they had seen him, they spread the word concerning what had been told them about this child, and all who heard it were amazed at what the shepherds said to them." (Luke 2:15-18)

They hurry to Bethlehem. Where do you find a manger? In a stable, of course. So they check out the stables in this village and come across one with a baby sleeping in it. They meet the Holy Family and share with them their story of the angelic visitation. Then they go and tell others what the angels have told them, just like the villagers did after the remarkable birth of John the Baptist (1:65). The NIV's translation "spread the word" seems to miss the point, which is rendered well in the KJV and NRSV: "They made known what had been told them about this child." The angel's announcement of "a savior, Christ the Lord" is spread throughout the area, resulting in amazement in the hearers.

Mary Ponders the Shepherd's Report (Luke 2:19)

> "But Mary treasured up all these things and pondered them in her heart." (Luke 2:19)

Mary has much to think about. "Treasured up" (NIV) or "kept all these things" (KJV) is *syntereō*, "to store information in one's mind for careful consideration, hold or treasure up (in one's memory)."[21] "Pondered" is *symballō*, "to give careful thought to, consider, ponder," something similar to our colloquial "get it all together."[22] She has a lot to process, a lot to make sense of. The shepherds do also.

Joyful Shepherds (Luke 2:20)

> "The shepherds returned, glorifying and praising God for all the things they had heard and seen, which were just as they had been told." (Luke 2:20)

The final scene in this passage finds the shepherds climbing back up the hill to where their flocks lie. The angel had told them what to expect and that's just the way they found it. We leave them glorifying (*doxazō*) and praising (*aineō*), the appropriate response to this unforgettable night.

Q5. (Luke 2:17-20) Great joy, praise, curiosity, amazement, telling others, thoughtful meditation. Which of these responses to the Good News are present in your life? In what manner do they show themselves? If some are missing, why? What can you do to recover these responses?
http://www.joyfulheart.com/forums/index.php?showtopic=723

---

[21] *Syntereō*, BDAG 975.
[22] *Symballō*, BDAG 956.

3. The Shepherds' Sign of the Manger (Luke 2:1-20)

Lessons for Disciples

What are we disciples supposed to get out of this telling of the story of Jesus' birth? Several things:

1. **God brings Good News to the poor and humble.** The shepherds, sometimes despised by their countrymen, were the first recipients of the Good News of Jesus' birth. Since God is no respecter of persons, we aren't to show favoritism either.
2. **The glory of the Lord is powerful and huge.** Just because we don't see it visibly doesn't mean that God isn't active. He often works in quiet ways. Only occasionally does he confirm his presence in miraculous ways.
3. Jesus is the **heir of David.**
4. Jesus is the expected **Savior, Messiah-Master-Lord-God** in our midst.
5. **The Good News is for all people**, Jew and Gentile alike.
6. **Not all people, however, receive God's peace**, but only those whom he has sovereignly chosen. Don't let suggestions of predestination trouble you. Be humble enough to allow God to be sovereign beyond your own meager understanding of these things. Deal with it! :-)
7. **Appropriate responses to this Good News** include "great joy" (2:10), praise (2:13-14, 20), curiosity to confirm its truth (2:15-16), amazement (2:18), telling others (2:17), and

thoughtful meditation (2:19). Nowhere do we see unbelief.

Prayer

Father, what an amazing night the shepherds had! To have a glimpse of your heavenly glory, to hear a mighty army chanting your praise, to see the Messiah-Child, to listen to the angel recite his glorious titles – Savior, Messiah, Lord. Thank you for letting us hear the story again. Write it large and indelibly in our hearts that we might be fervent Good News tellers, too. In Jesus' name, we pray. Amen.

Key Verses

> "And she gave birth to her firstborn, a son. She wrapped him in cloths and placed him in a manger, because there was no room for them in the inn" (Luke 2:7)

> "For unto you is born this day in the city of David a Savior, which is Christ the Lord." (Luke 2:11, KJV)

4. Wise Men and the Christmas Star of Bethlehem (Matthew 2:1-12)

150 years ago John H. Hopkins, Jr. penned the words and music of this haunting carol of the wise men:

"We three kings of Orient are bearing gifts, we traverse afar..."

"The Journey of the Magi" (1894) by James Jacques Joseph Tissot (French painter and illustrator, 1836-1902), oil on canvas, Minneapolis Institute of Arts.

They weren't kings. We're pretty sure of that. Nor were there necessarily three of them. Nor did they go by the names Caspar, Melchior and Balthasar.[1] But who were they and why did they come? How do they fit into the story of Jesus' infancy?

---

[1] These names for the Magi in the West derive from an early 6th century Greek manuscript. However Eastern churches and Armenians have different names for them.

Who Are the Magi? (Matthew 2:1)

Let's follow the story as Matthew tells it:

> "After Jesus was born in Bethlehem in Judea, during the time of King Herod, Magi from the east came to Jerusalem and asked, 'Where is the one who has been born king of the Jews? We saw his star in the east and have come to worship him.'" (Matthew 2:1-2)

All of a sudden an elaborate entourage from the East appears in Jerusalem at Herod's court inquiring about the birth of the "King of the Jews."

These men are described as "Wise men" (NRSV, KJV) or "Magi" (NIV). The word is *magos*, "a (Persian, then also Babylonian) wise man and priest, who was expert in astrology, interpretation of dreams, and various other occult arts."[2]

Where were they from? The text says "the east" (*anatolē*), the direction from which the sun rises. Where could that be? There are three main possibilities:

1. **Parthia or Persia.** The term *magoi* was first associated with the Medes and the Persians. We know that astrology flourished in this area and that the astral lore of the region was applied to royal births.

---

[2] *Magos*, BDAG 608. Good discussions are included in Brown, *Birth*, 167 and Gerhard Delling, *magos, ktl.*, TDNT 4:356-59.

2. **Babylon.** The Babylonians or Chaldeans had a well developed interest in astronomy and astrology. A large colony of Jews remained there, so astrologers could have learned of Jewish messianic expectations. Also, *magoi* are referred to in Daniel's description of the Babylonian court.
3. **Arabia or the Syrian desert.** The gifts of gold, frankincense, and myrrh are associated with desert camel trains coming from Midian in northwest Arabia or Sheba in southwest Arabia. Astrology was not unknown and Jewish colonies existed in various cities.[3]

Which of these is most likely? We can't really say. At any rate, they were men of wisdom and learning from an exotic, far away land bringing a caravan into the capital city of the Jews, seeking a newborn king. They must have attracted attention.

What Kind of "Star" Did They See? (Matthew 2:2)

> "... and asked, 'Where is the one who has been born king of the Jews? We saw his star in the east and have come to worship him.'" (Matthew 2:2)

"Star" (*astēr*) wasn't used in a modern scientific sense. Rather it referred to "a luminous body (other than the sun) visible in the sky, star, single star,

---

[3] Brown, *Birth*, pp. 168-170.

planet."[4] Foerster notes, "*Astēr* almost always denotes a single "star," whereas *astron* can also be used for a "constellation."[5] The phrase "in the east" (NIV, KJV, *anatolē*) in verses 2 and 9 may well carry the meaning "at its rising" (NRSV), of the "upward movement of celestial bodies."[6]

Here are some of the possibilities:

1. **A supernova or "new star."** A supernova is an explosion in an existing star that for several weeks or months gives out a great deal of light, sometimes even visible during the day. A dozen novae are discovered each year, but those visible to the naked eye are rare. There is no historical record of a supernova just before Jesus' birth date.
2. **A comet.** Throughout history, comets have captured human imagination. A comet's nucleus is made up of rock, dust, and ices. Its tail can be spectacular. The sun's radiation pressure and solar wind cause an very long tail to form, which points away from the sun. Astronomers have calculated that Halley's comet would have been visible 12-11 BC, years before Jesus' birth about 6 BC.
3. **A planetary conjunction.** Astrologers pay attention to the planets. Apparently there was

---

[4] *Astēr*, BDAG 145.
[5] Werner Foerster, *astēr, astron*, TDNT 1:503-505.
[6] *Anatolē*, BDAG 74.

4. Wise Men and Star of Bethlehem (Matthew 2:1-12)

> a conjunction of Jupiter, Saturn, and Mars that occurred in 7-6 BC, and mention seems to have been made of this in cuneiform texts. Some have gone farther. This series of conjunctions over several months took place in the zodiacal constellation of Pisces, which may have been associated with the last days and with the Hebrews. Jupiter was associated with the world ruler among Parthian astrologers. Saturn was identified as the star of the Amorites of the Syrian-Palestine region. These three indicators could have pointed to a world ruler among the Hebrews in the last days. But this is purely speculative, astrology by hindsight. Nor do we have any evidence that such a conjunction of planets would have been actually referred to as a "star."[7]

We just don't know enough to say authoritatively exactly what the Star of Bethlehem was.

There is a star spoken of in prophecy, however, in a prophecy of Balaam, the errant prophet:

> "I see him, but not now;
> I behold him, but not near.
> A star will come out of Jacob;
> a scepter will rise out of Israel." (Numbers 24:17)

The initial reference seems to be to David. Prior to Christ, Jews of the Qumran community saw this

---

[7] Brown, *Birth*, pp. 171-173.

prophecy as messianic. Later Judaism considered the messianic claims of Simon bar Kochba ("son of the star," 132-135 AD).[8] Could the messianic expectation based on this verse among Jewish communities in the East be the basis of the Magi's interpretation of the star? We don't know.

Q1. (Matthew 2:1-2; Numbers 24:17) What is the significance of the Star of Bethlehem that the Magi saw? Why do you think the Magi came to find the Christ-child when they saw the star? In what way was does prophecy prefigure this event?
http://www.joyfulheart.com/forums/index.php?showtopic=724

Why Was Herod Disturbed? (Matthew 2:3)

"When King Herod heard this he was disturbed, and all Jerusalem with him." (Matthew 2:3)

A delegation of important people coming to Jerusalem to honor the king or to worship in the temple wouldn't be uncommon. But the Magi's search for a

---

[8] Brown, *Birth*, p. 195, fn. 47 gives references to the Qumran literature. See also R.K. Harrison, *Numbers* (Baker, 1992), pp. 321-324. In the book of Revelation Jesus says, "I am the Root and the Offspring of David, and the bright Morning Star" (Revelation 22:16). On the Messianic expectation in later Judaism, Foerster (TDNT 1:505) cites Strack and Billerback I, 13c, 17f.

newborn king based on an astronomical phenomenon caused quite a stir. The passive of *tarassō* means to "be troubled, frightened, terrified."[9]

Herod was troubled because he saw this newborn as a threat to his own throne. The people were troubled because they had seen what their paranoid king had done when he felt his throne threatened. A later Roman philosopher quotes Roman emperor Caesar Augustus as joking "I'd rather be Herod's sow than Herod's son."[10] Herod didn't eat pigs, but he murdered his sons. Afraid of intrigue among his many sons to become king, two were tried and executed by strangulation just the year before Jesus' birth – about 7 BC. A third was executed five days before Herod's death in 4 BC.[11]

Matthew's report of both Herod and his citizens being "disturbed" at the Magi's report rings true.

Where Was the Messiah to Be Born? (Matthew 2:4-6)

Herod takes the Magi's quest seriously.

> "When he had called together all the people's chief priests and teachers of the law, he asked them where the Christ was to be born.' In Bethlehem in Judea,' they replied, 'for this is what the prophet has written:

---

[9] *Tarassō*, BDAG 990-991.
[10] Abrosius Theodosius Macrobius, *The Saturnalia*. Macrobius was a Roman philosopher of the fourth century AD.
[11] Josephus, *Antiquities*, xvi.10.6-11.8; *Wars* i.27.1-6. Harold W. Hoehner, "Herod," ISBE 2:688-698.

> "But you, Bethlehem, in the land of Judah,
> are by no means least among the rulers of Judah;
> for out of you will come a ruler
> who will be the shepherd of my people Israel."'"
> (Matthew 2:4-6)

Note that the Magi came seeking "the one who has been born king of the Jews" (2:1), but Herod asked the scholars where the Messiah (Greek *Christos*) would be born (2:4). He understood immediately that this child they sought was no normal king, but the Messiah himself.

Herod wasn't a descendent of David. He was rather a Edomite (Idumean) son of a ruling family in whom the Romans had seen a talent for controlling the populace. He had been appointed governor of Galilee (47 BC) and later King of the Jews (37 BC). He realized that if a descendent of David were to rise, his reign and that of his descendents would be over. Messiah or not, this child must be destroyed.

Herod's Plot (Matthew 2:7-8)

The prophet Micah had made it clear that Bethlehem would be the birthplace of the Messiah (Micah 5:2), so in Bethlehem the quest would continue.

> "Then Herod called the Magi secretly and found out from them the exact time the star had appeared. He sent them to Bethlehem and said, 'Go and make a careful search for the child. As soon as you find him, report to me, so that I too may go and worship him.'" (Matthew 2:7-8)

Herod's questioning of the scholars was public, but his interrogation of the Magi is secret.[12] He finds out precisely[13] when the star appeared. Later he uses this information to slaughter all the boy babies in Bethlehem two years and under (2:16). Apparently the Magi had seen the sign two years previous.

Now Herod seeks to enlist the Magi as his secret agents: "As soon as you find him, report to me...." (2:8) He claims to desire to worship the newborn Messiah, but his real desire is assassination. "Worship" (NIV, KJV) or "pay homage" (NRSV) is *proskyneō*, literally, "kiss towards." It means "to express in attitude or gesture one's complete dependence on or submission to a high authority figure, (fall down and) worship, do obeisance to, prostrate oneself before, do reverence to, welcome respectfully."[14]

Led by the Star (Matthew 2:9-10)

> "After they had heard the king, they went on their way, and the star they had seen in the east went ahead of them until it stopped over the place where the child was. When they saw the star, they were overjoyed." (Matthew 2:9-10)

It seems that they had seen the star "at its rising" (or "in the East") and had come to Jerusalem, since that is where they expected to find a newborn King of

---

[12] *Lathra*, "without others being aware, secretly" (BDAG 581).
[13] *Akriboō*, "make detailed inquiry about something, ascertain precisely/exactly" (BDAG 39).
[14] *Proskyneō*, BDAG 882-883.

the Jews. But now the star, which seems to have disappeared for a while, now reappears and "went ahead of them." *Proagō* means "to move ahead or in front of, go before, lead the way, precede."[15] Finally it "stopped" (NIV, NRSV) or "stood" (KJV) over the place where the child was." *Histēmi*, "set, place," here means "to desist from movement and be in a stationary position, stand still, stop."[16]

The star that inspired their trip in the first place now leads them directly to the very home where the Christ-child dwelt.

Worshipping the King (Matthew 2:11a)

> "On coming to the house, they saw the child with his mother Mary, and they bowed down and worshiped him." (Matthew 2:11a)

By this time, presumably nearly two years after Jesus' birth, Mary and Joseph were living in a house (*oikia*[17]). While most nativity scenes have shepherds bumping into wise men and angels, this almost certainly was not the case. The Holy Family had left the stable and found a house. Probably Joseph had found employment as a carpenter. They had apparently decided not to return to Nazareth, perhaps because of the scandal over Mary's pregnancy prior to marriage. Even though Joseph publicly accepted the child as his own, premarital relations were

---

[15] *Proagō*, BDAG 864, 2a.
[16] *Histēmi*, BDAG 482-483, B1.
[17] *Oikia*, "a structure used as a dwelling, house" (BDAG 695, 1a).

4. Wise Men and Star of Bethlehem (Matthew 2:1-12)

considered a sin; the couple would have had to deal with considerable prejudice.

But now, outside their home, a caravan of exotic travelers has stopped. Strangely dressed men are approaching while their camels are attended by servants, while other servants are carrying gifts in their hands. Mary scurries around to straighten up while Joseph goes out to meet the strangers.

We're not told the details, of course, but when the Magi see the child, now a toddler, they bow down (*piptō*[18]) and worship (*proskuneō*) him.

Rembrandt, detail of "The Adoration of the Magi" (1632), Oil on paper pasted on canvas, 45x39 cm, Hermitage Museum, St. Petersburg.

Imagine these old men, finely dressed, prostrating themselves on a dirt floor before a small child. They had seen the star and it had reappeared to guide them. These men were convinced – rightly – that they were standing before the Messiah, the King of the Jews. Their obeisance was fitting.

---

[18] *Piptō*, "fall," here, to "fall down, throw oneself to the ground" as a sign of devotion or humility, before high-ranking persons or divine beings, especially when one approaches with a petition. (BDAG 815-816, 1bא).

> Q2. (Matthew 2:11a) What do we learn from seeing the Magi prostrating themselves before the child Jesus? What was the significance of this for them? How can we emulate this kind of worship?
> http://www.joyfulheart.com/forums/index.php?showtopic=725

Offering Gifts to the King (Matthew 2:11b)

After lying prostrate for some time, they rise, perhaps at the urging of Joseph.

> "Then they opened their treasures and presented him with gifts of gold and of incense and of myrrh." (Matthew 2:11b)

Whenever foreign dignitaries would appear before a great king they would bring gifts as a sign of obeisance and honor. "Treasures" (NIV, KJV) is probably better translated "treasure chests" (NRSV).[19] And as the lids were lifted, the glitter of gold and aroma of precious spices filled the room.

1. **Gold**, of course, was the most precious and valued metal known. It was highly prized. It was not found in Palestine, but had to be im-

---

[19] *Thēsauros*, "a place where something is kept for safekeeping, repository ... treasure box or chest." It can also mean that which is stored up, "treasure," but the context of opening here suggests the chest. We get our English word "thesaurus" from this word (BDAG 456).

4. Wise Men and Star of Bethlehem (Matthew 2:1-12)

ported from the mines of Ophir and elsewhere.[20]

2. **Frankincense** is derived from three species of the genus *Boswellia* – *B. carterii*, *B. papyri-fera*, and *B. thurifera* – which grow in southern Arabia, India, and elsewhere. The gum is exuded from the incised bark in pale glittering drops. It had a bitter flavor and a strong balsamic odor when heated. The Egyptians used it for fumigation and embalming; the Israelites used it in worship in the Holy Place of the tabernacle and temple (Exodus 30:34).[21]

3. **Myrrh** is valuable as a perfume and a constituent of sacred anointing oil (Exodus 30:23). Several shrubs produce a perfumed resinous substance described as myrrh, but the one compounded in the anointing oil was probably from *Commiphora myrrha* or perhaps *Balsamodendron myrrha*, a low thorny tree distributed across south Arabia and Ethiopia. The sap is pleasantly scented and dries into a solid resin. It could be diluted to form a liquid cosmetic product and may have been used by Egyptians in embalming.[22]

These may seem inappropriate gifts for a baby, but as munificent gifts from distinguished personages

---

[20] George A. Turner and Ralph W. Vunderink, "Gold," ISBE 2:520-522.
[21] R.K. Harrison, "Frankincense," ISBE 2:360.
[22] R.K. Harrison, "Myrrh," ISBE 3:450-451.

appearing before a king, they would be considered quite appropriate, perhaps as specimens of the products of their country.[23] Later Christian writers, including John H. Hopkins, Jr. who wrote "We Three Kings," have seen significance in gold for Christ's royalty, frankincense for his deity, and myrrh for his humanity, ultimately his burial, though none of this is in Matthew's account.[24] I can't help think of the song "The Little Drummer Boy" (1958):

> "I have no gift to bring ...
> that's fit to give the King ...
> I played my drum for Him ...
> I played my best for Him ...
> Then He smiled at me ... me and my drum."[25]

The song is popular, though the sentiment is profound. Our best, no matter how seemingly insignificant, is what we owe the King. That is what characterized the Magi's gifts.

Though the Magi's quest had brought Herod's scrutiny upon the child, these gifts were probably sold gradually to provide for the Holy Family during three years of exile in Egypt where they fled to escape Herod's wrath.

---

[23] Edersheim, *Life and Times* 1:214.
[24] Edersheim, *Life and Times* 1:214, fn. 1.
[25] "The Little Drummer Boy," by Katherine K. Davis, Henry Onorati and Harry Simeone. Copyright ©1958, EMI Mills Music Inc., International Korwin Corp. (ASCAP).

> Q3. (Matthew 2:11b) Why was it appropriate for the Magi bring gifts to the Christ-child? How does the extravagance of their gifts reflect their heart attitude? What kinds of gifts are appropriate for us to bring?
> http://www.joyfulheart.com/forums/index.php?showtopic=726

Disobeying Herod (Matthew 2:12)

> "And having been warned in a dream not to go back to Herod, they returned to their country by another route." (Matthew 2:12)

Though Herod had recruited the Magi for his evil plot, God warned them in a dream not to participate, so they left the area without returning through Jerusalem, only six miles to the north. This probably bought the Holy Family a day or two of time to make good their escape.

The story concludes in Matthew 2:13-23 with Joseph being warned in a dream and that very night taking his young family – with the treasures – and fleeing for Egypt, out of Herod's jurisdiction and reach. It was good that they did flee rather than question God's messenger. As soon as Herod discovered that the Magi had betrayed him, in a furious rage he gave orders to kill all the male children in Bethlehem who were two years of age or under. This amounted to perhaps twenty baby boys, the first martyrs for the Messiah.

What Does All this Mean?

Why does Matthew include the story of the wise men in his Gospel? There were many incidents that he chose to exclude that we find, for example, in Luke's and John's gospels. I see in this account several themes:

1. **The King Heralded by a Star**. Matthew points to the fulfillment (without saying so) of Balaam's ancient prophecy that "A star will come forth from Jacob, and a scepter will rise from Israel" (Numbers 24:17).
2. **The King Honored by Foreign Nations**. One of Matthew's themes is that Christ fulfilled Old Testament prophecy. Here the prophecy isn't cited, but only alluded to: that of foreign rulers bringing their riches to honor the King of Israel (1 Kings 10:2, 10; Psalm 72:10-11, 15; Isaiah 60:5-6, 11). This account points to Jesus' royalty as King of the Jews.
3. **Enemies of Christ Seek His Death**. Here in chapter 2 is the beginning of Jesus' enemies. Herod clearly covets Jesus' claim to be Messiah and seeks to kill him before he can become a threat. Later in Matthew's gospel the

"chief priests and teachers of the law" who pointed to his birthplace in Bethlehem conspire to take his life. And ultimately he is crucified for this very charge of being King of the Jews.[1]
4. **Explanation of Jesus' Infant Sojourns.** From Nazareth to Bethlehem, from Bethlehem to Egypt, and then back to Nazareth where he was raised – Jesus' journeys as an infant needed an explanation in the face of Jewish belittling him as a citizen of Nazareth (John 1:45-46), not from the royal city of Bethlehem.

The Gospel to the Gentiles. This account also points to another important theme – that Jesus came to the Jews, but had a mission beyond Israel to the Gentiles.[2] In parable (Matthew 21:33-44; 22:2-13), action (Matthew 8:5-13), prophecy (Matthew 24:14), and command (Matthew 28:19; Acts 1:8), Jesus underscores that the gospel must be preached to – and will be embraced by – the Gentiles.

---

[1] Matthew 27:11, 37; John 18:33-37; 19:19-22.
[2] Genesis 12:3; 22:18; 28:14; 49:10; Psalm 22:27; 98:3; Isaiah 49:6; 66:19.

5.

> Q4. Read Matthew 8:5-13; 21:33-44; 22:2-13; 24:14; and 28:19. What do they have in common? What relation does the visit of the wise men have to Matthew's theme of bringing the Gospel to the Gentiles? How should we be applying this mandate in our own lives?
> http://www.joyfulheart.com/forums/index.php?showtopic=727

6. **Devotion by Men of Wisdom**. That wise men recognize the Messiah and bow at his feet is also an example to "the wisdom of this world" (1 Corinthians 2:6).
7. **The Sovereignty of God**. Finally, we see in Joseph an obedient servant of God, who hears the angel's warnings in dreams and takes immediate action to protect the Christ-child in his charge. Though the powers of this world may array themselves against the Christ and his people, God is fully able of protecting and preserving them until they have completed their mission. The gifts of the wise men serve to honor the boy-King and to provide for his

shelter for years to come. Where one door closes, another opens. God provides!

Prayer

Father, thank you for letting us hear the story of the Magi who knelt before you with devotion and brought you rich gifts. Let us have that kind of wisdom, that we may bring before you extravagant worship and offer back to you the gifts you have given to us. We love you, Lord Jesus. In your holy name, we pray. Amen.

Key Verses

"After Jesus was born in Bethlehem in Judea, during the time of King Herod, Magi from the east came to Jerusalem and asked, 'Where is the one who has been born king of the Jews? We saw his star in the east and have come to worship him.'" (Matthew 2:1-2)

"On coming to the house, they saw the child with his mother Mary, and they bowed down and worshiped him. Then they opened their treasures and presented him with gifts of gold and of incense and of myrrh." (Matthew 2:11)

Appendix: Class Handouts

In this section you'll find the discussion questions. Since you are the paid owner of this book, you are free to print out the class or group handouts without any further payment.

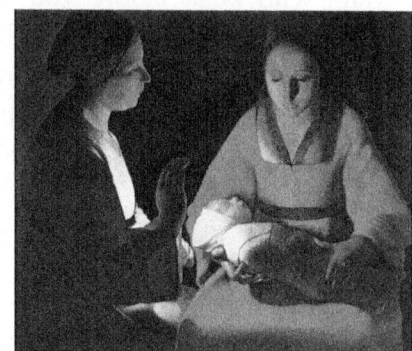

Georges de la Tour (1593-1652), "The Newborn" (1640s), Oil on canvas, 76 x 91 cm, Musée des Beaux-Arts, Rennes.

1. Mary, the Virgin Mother (Luke 1:26-45)
2. Joseph, the Stand-In Father (Matthew 1:18-25)
3. The Shepherds' Sign of the Manger (Luke 2:1-20)
4. Wise Men and the Christmas Star of Bethlehem (Matthew 2:1-12)

1. Mary, the Virgin Mother (Luke 1:26-45)

The points of this announcement.
- Mary will become pregnant.
- Mary will give birth to a son.
- The child must be given the name "Jesus" (see Matthew 1:21).
- The child will become a great person.
- His title will be "Son of the Most High."

He will inherit "the throne of his father David, and he will reign over the house of Jacob forever," in other words, he will be the long anticipated King of the Jews, the Jewish Messiah, the "Son of David," who will reign over the Kingdom of God.

Finally, "his kingdom will never end."

Discussion Questions:

Q1. (Luke 1:31-34) What did the angel's announcement say about who Mary's Child was and who he was to become?

Q2. (Luke 1:34) In what way does Mary's "How?" question (1:34) to the angel's declaration differ from Zechariah's "How?" question (1:18)? Why was Mary rewarded and Zechariah disciplined?

Q3. (Luke 1:35) What does the virgin conception teach us about Jesus' nature? How central is the doctrine of the virgin conception to the Christian message?

Q4. (Luke 1:38) What is the essence of Mary's positive response to the angel? What can we learn from her response for our own lives? In what sense was Mary's response an "informed consent"? When we respond to God, what do we consent to?

Q5. (Luke 1:42-43) In what sense are the titles "Blessed Virgin Mary" and "Mother of God" appropriate for Mary? Why are we sometimes hesitant to exalt her as "blessed among women"?

2. Joseph, the Stand-In Father (Matthew 1:18-25)

Q1. What would Jesus have learned as the son of a carpenter? What experiences would this have exposed him to?

Mary's pregnancy had placed her at considerable risk in this society:

1. **Husband**. Her betrothed husband would reject her.
2. **Penalty**. At worst she could be stoned (Deuteronomy 22:13-30).
3. **Shunning**. She and her bastard child would be shunned.
4. **Remarriage**. The stigma of her supposed adultery would remain with her and taint the reputation of any husband.
5. **Nowhere to go**.

Q2. (Matthew 1:19) What were Mary's options being pregnant and carrying a baby not her husband's? What kind of character did Joseph exhibit by deciding to divorce Mary quietly and leniently?

Q3. (Matthew 1:21) What is the significance of the name Jesus? Why do you think the angel gave the name to both Mary (Luke 1:31) and Joseph independently?

Prophecy in the Old Testament takes several shapes, including:

1. **Exhortation**, a directive word from God to a particular person or people at a particular time.
2. **Prediction**, a clear foretelling of the future for a person or nation.
3. **Acted prophecy** (Hosea 1:2).
4. **Foreshadowing**, where a contemporary prophetic event or insight foreshadows a distant one, so there is a double fulfillment – a present-time fulfillment (the type) and a future completion (the antitype) which brings the prophecy to fullness or completion.

Q4. (Matthew 1:23) How did the prophetic concept of the virgin conception and the name "Immanuel" find their fullness in the birth of Jesus to Mary?

Q5. (1:24-25) What does Joseph accepting Mary as his wife say about his character? What is the significance for prophetic fulfillment of Jesus as a Son of David that Joseph "named" the child "Jesus"?

3. The Shepherds' Sign of the Manger (Luke 2:1-20)

Q1. (Luke 2:1-2) Why does Luke name the rulers in 2:1-2? What point is he making?

Q2. Why do you think the journey to Bethlehem was difficult for Mary? Is pleasure an indication that we are in God's will or not? Any examples from your life? Extra Credit: Argue for or against this proposition: "Being a consistent Christian causes more hardships than just going with the flow."

Q3. (Luke 2:7-8) Why do you think the message of Jesus' birth comes to shepherds, of all people? Why is Jesus born in a stable with a manger for a bed? This has to be intentional. What point is God making?

Q4. (Luke 2:11) What are the three titles of Jesus given by the angels? What does each mean? What does this tell us about Jesus' true identity?

Q5. (Luke 2:17-20) Great joy, praise, curiosity, amazement, telling others, thoughtful meditation. Which of these responses to the Good News are present in your life? In what manner do they show themselves? If some are missing, why? What can you do to recover these responses?

What are we disciples supposed to get out of this telling of the story of Jesus' birth? Several things:

1. **God brings Good News to the poor and humble.** The shepherds, sometimes despised by their countrymen, were the first recipients of the Good News of Jesus' birth. Since God is no respecter of persons, we aren't to show favoritism either.
2. **The glory of the Lord is powerful and huge.** Just because we don't see it visibly doesn't mean that God isn't active. He often works in quiet ways. Only occasionally does he confirm his presence in miraculous ways.
3. Jesus is the **heir of David.**
4. Jesus is the expected **Savior, Messiah-Master-Lord-God** in our midst.
5. **The Good News is for all people**, Jew and Gentile alike.
6. **Not all people, however, receive God's peace**, but only those whom he has sovereignly chosen.
7. **Appropriate responses to this Good News** include "great joy" (2:10), praise (2:13-14, 20), curiosity to confirm its truth (2:15-16), amazement (2:18), telling others (2:17), and thoughtful meditation (2:19). Nowhere do we see unbelief.

4. Wise Men and the Christmas Star of Bethlehem (Matthew 2:1-12)

Where did the wise men come from? The text says "the east" (*anatolē*), the direction from which the sun rises. There are three main possibilities:

1. Parthia or Persia.
2. Babylon
3. Arabia or the Syrian desert

What kind of "star" did they see? We don't know for sure. Possibilities include:

1. A supernova or "new star"
2. A comet
3. A planetary conjunction

Q1. (Matthew 2:1-2; Numbers 24:17) What is the significance of the Star of Bethlehem that the Magi saw? Why do you think the Magi came to find the Christ-child when they saw the star? In what way was does prophecy prefigure this event?

Q2. (Matthew 2:11a) What do we learn from seeing the Magi prostrating themselves before the child Jesus? What was the significance of this for them? How can we emulate this kind of worship?

Q3. (Matthew 2:11b) Why was it appropriate for the Magi bring gifts to the Christ-child? How does the extravagance of their gifts reflect their heart attitude? What kinds of gifts are appropriate for us to bring?

Q4. Read Matthew 8:5-13; 21:33-44; 22:2-13; 24:14; and 28:19. What do they have in common? What relation does the visit of the wise men have to Matthew's theme of bringing the Gospel to the Gentiles? How should we be applying this mandate in our own lives?

This passage has several themes:
1. The King Heralded by a Star (Numbers 24:17)
2. The King Honored by Foreign Nations (1 Kings 10:2, 10; Psalm 72:10-11, 15; Isaiah 60:5-6, 11)
3. Enemies of Christ Seek His Death (Matthew 27:11, 37; John 18:33-37; 19:19-22)
4. Explanation of Jesus' Infant Sojourns
5. The Gospel to the Gentiles (Genesis 12:3; 22:18; 28:14; 49:10; Psalm 22:27; 98:3; Isaiah 49:6; 66:19; Matthew 21:33-44; 22:2-13; 8:5-13; 24:14; Matthew 28:19; Acts 1:8)
6. Devotion by Men of Wisdom (1 Corinthians 2:6)
7. The Sovereignty of God

CPSIA information can be obtained at www.ICGtesting.com
Printed in the USA
BVOW11s2323071115

425663BV00001B/13/P